BILLBOARD MONUMENTS

of

MAINE

A Collection of Rare 1800s Gravestones

RON ROMANO

Designed and produced by:
Indie Author Books
12 High Street, Thomaston, Maine
www.indieauthorbooks.com

Printed in the United States of America

For all of the wonderful work they do,
this book is dedicated to:

The Maine Old Cemetery Association
&
The Association for Gravestone Studies

CONTENTS

ACKNOWLEDGMENTS

Creating this book has been an interesting and enjoyable journey that allowed me to interact with many folks from both MOCA (the Maine Old Cemetery Association) and AGS (the Association for Gravestone Studies). For those who sent pictures, offered leads, supplied information, and joined me in getting excited about this "new" form of grave marker, I thank you!

A dozen people (a baker's dozen, really) went the extra mile and deserve these extra words of appreciation: Abby Burnett, Craig Stinson, and Teresa Harris, all of Arkansas, provided me with a great deal of information about the fascinating Hill and Sargent families of Yarmouth. I also owe a debt of gratitude to my friends from MOCA, who helped promote my quest to find billboards and supplied pictures of some that I didn't know about: Perri Black, Jess Couture, Debi Curry, Janet Mahannah, Angela Tibbetts, and Cheryl Willis Patten. I so appreciated Debbie Allen Grover's invitation to present my research to Maine's cemetery directors at the 2019 annual meeting of the Maine Cemetery Association, and subsequently Sonny Perkins's invitation to meet in Ogunquit so he could show me firsthand the work he did to preserve the billboard monument there. Art Gaffar, historian at the Maine Charitable Mechanic Association, is my go-to guy regarding Maine's early tradesmen, and once again he didn't disappoint. And for helping me measure and photograph all of the billboards found along

Maine's coast south of Portland, I owe a few more coffees to my long-time friend Tricia Granzier.

While I'm the author of the book, I know from past experience that it takes a village to get from vision to reality. To all of the following, who helped me find monuments, offer guidance, and provide general help, thank you for being my village people! John Babin, Bruce Blanchard, Colleen Sanders Broyles, Kit Burdick, Karen Caton-Locke, John C. Carter, Mary and Sonny Chipman, Flossie Dere, Diane Del Favero Holden, Steve Dow, Bob Drinkwater, Ruth Fernandez, Joe Ferrannini, Laurel Gabel, Susan Tupper Gillmor, Janice Gower, Dawn Hackett, Don Hamlin, Bill Harding, Linda Heald, Jan Hill, Wayne Hoar, Sam Howes, Jonathan Kewley, Seth Koren, Tiffany Link, Charlie Marchant, Ed Mendes, Francis Miller, Pat Moening, Dennis Montagna, Deborah Nelson, Nick Noyes, Deb Probert, Wynona Randall, Jamie Rice, Yvonne Richard, Ashlynn Rickord, Leslie Rounds, Roland Rhoades, Kathy Ostrander Roberts, JoAnne Russo, Kimberly J. Sawtelle, Charlie Smith, Adam Strout, Anne Tait, Michael Updike, Dale and Tina Utter, Kenneth White, Patti Whitten, Katie Worthing, Martha Zimicki, and, of course, my ever-supportive spouse, Chuck.

INTRODUCTION

*V*isit a Maine burying ground from the 1700s and you'll likely find a winged skull staring vacantly back at you. Those "death's heads" were the most common decoration on the gray slate grave markers imported from Massachusetts at the time. By the early 1800s, the flow of Massachusetts-made gravestones had virtually ended, as stonecutters such as Bartlett Adams (in Portland by 1800) and Sullivan Dwight (in Thomaston in 1810) established successful businesses supplying locals with their own finely carved slate and marble markers. More pleasant images such as human faces, urns and willows, and flowers were the designs this new generation of gravestone makers carved onto stone. By the early 1900s, cemeteries became filled with machine-cut granite, as hand-carved grave markers had by then been largely abandoned. Now, in the early 2000s, we find cemeteries introducing columbaria to their landscapes in order to meet the increasing demand for cremation.

1840 TO 1860: A REMARKABLE PERIOD OF CHANGE

While much has changed in Maine's cemeteries in 300 years, perhaps the most remarkable period of transition occurred during the mid-nineteenth century. The gray slate that had been in use since the early 1700s was no longer preferred; instead, white marble reigned supreme. Given its relative softness, marble allowed gravestone carvers to show their artistic flair with beautiful, three-dimensional designs. Stone shop ads of this period reflect this change; many gravestone makers altogether omitted "slate" from their product lists. They advertised marble and referred to themselves as "marble workers" instead of "stone cutters." By 1850, there was a great deal of competition in this trade. The 1856 *Maine Register and Business Directory* listed 44 marble workers from 32 towns. Many decades later, we gravestone researchers benefit from that competition. The signatures marble workers carved onto their monuments—intended at the time to advertise their work to the general public—now serve as aids to those of us who wish to study the work of a particular carver or shop.

In this period, the use of footstones also fell from common use. During the earlier "slate age," most people purchased a pair of gravestones: a headstone (usually large, fully decorated and inscribed) with an accompanying footstone (usually much

Marble Workers.	
Foss James,	Auburn
Nevins Samuel,	"
Pullen G. & C.,	Augusta
Bradbury S. P.,	Bangor
Thaxter Joshua H.,	"
Turner W. H.,	Bath
Cook Charles M.,	"
Wright J.,	"
Jones & Stevens,	Belfast
Lord E.,	Biddeford
Smith Richard,	Bridgton
Adams Arthur,	Brunswick
Sawyer & Robbins,	Calais
Clark Andrew E.,	Camden
Smith H. R., (A. P. O.)	Danville
Soule G. T.,	Farmington
Osgood E. G.,	Fryeburg
Park S. J. & Co.,	Gardiner
Berry R. P.,	Kennebunk
Elder G.,	Gorham
McLellan S. E.,	"
Whitney Ezra A.,	Freeman
Smith Samuel,	Hallowell
Thompson Ira,	Newfield
Brigham Elbridge G.,	Paris
Hunt & Jewett,	Portland
Parker L.,	"
Thompson Joseph R.,	"
Watts Freeman J.,	Prescott
Cobb & Mather,	Rockland
Cleaves John,	Saco
Emery John F.,	"
Baker, Emery, & Co.,	Skowhegan
Coburn & Hill,	South Berwick
Rollins William H.,	Standish
Edgarton Otis,	Thomaston
Watts H. L.,	Wales
Glidden J. P.,	Waldoboro'
Estes Joseph,	Westbrook
Stevens W. A. F.,	Waterville

Marble workers in Maine in 1856.

smaller, inscribed only with initials and a date). The pair marked the borders of the grave and with their inscribed sides facing outward, visitors could easily see who was buried in the plot without stepping on it. Later, in the midcentury, people tended toward purchasing a single stone placed at the head of the grave, and with this change came one more: headstones were usually oriented so that the inscriptions faced inward to the grave instead of outward from it.

RISE OF THE RURAL CEMETERY

These changes were influenced by the rural (or garden) cemetery movement introduced in 1831 with the dedication of the 175-acre Mount Auburn Cemetery in Cambridge, Massachusetts. Soon after, in 1834, the movement reached Maine with the establishment of Bangor's 300-acre Mount Hope Cemetery. Others that followed include the 170-acre Laurel Hill Cemetery in Saco (1844) and the 240-acre Evergreen Cemetery in Deering (now Portland) in 1855. Rural cemeteries offered visitors rolling landscapes with attractive shrubs and trees, water features, and flower gardens. They were designed to be beautiful public spaces and encouraged visitors to picnic, stroll, and enjoy their natural surroundings (while getting in a little bit of time for mourning lost loved ones, of course…).

The design of rural cemeteries offered an alternative to the colonial practice of packing as many bodies as possible into the burial patch. In those utilitarian burying grounds and church yards located in older New England towns, bodies were usually laid in long straight lines. Furthermore, before rural cemeteries, the deceased were almost always buried using a "head to the west, feet to the east" orientation, to allow their resurrected souls to rise (as if from bed) to greet the dawn. The rural cemeteries left straight-line burials behind, and instead were created with winding pathways encircling attractive patches of land that allowed bodies to be buried to fit the landscape. Later in the century, while addressing the Connecticut Board of Agriculture on the subject of rural cemeteries, Rev. John DePeu remarked, "Fortunately we have gotten rid of the old idea that the dead must all have their heels toward the east so that they may rise up facing the Lord at His coming. Now we put them either way and believe they will find the Lord's face when He comes. So we are able to lay out grounds in properly diversified fashion."[1]

Well-to-do citizens bought the best plots in the best spots in garden cemeteries and decorated them grandly with impressive mausoleums, beautiful statues, and large monuments. These popular midcentury landscapes offered the growing number of marble workers an opportunity to show the public their abilities as sculptors of stone, and a great variety of shapes and sizes of white marble monuments filled the lots and plots of our cemeteries, large and small.

Among all of these changes, a new type of monument began to appear: a unique design comprised of large rectangular marble slabs and granite posts that, when put together, resembled signboards more than gravestones. Though rarely found and often overlooked today, these monuments enrich the fabric of Maine's cemeteries. Whether for their interesting construction, the stories of those they memorialize, or their makers, this book shines a spotlight on these monuments and helps tell the story of Maine's past.

- Note 1: Every known Maine billboard is included in this book. When describing them I provide general size information for context, since photographs alone can be deceptive in that regard. See the Appendix for exact dimensions, stone weights, construction details, production dates, and notes about each billboard's physical condition.
- Note 2: I use the words "stone," "gravestone," "marker," "grave marker," and "monument" throughout the book to describe the memorial stones found in our cemeteries. I use all of those words, plus "billboard" and "family billboard," to describe the particular monuments that are the subject of this book.
- Note 3: When I say midcentury, I am specifically referring to the period of time in which the majority of these monuments were made: 1845 to 1870.

---

1. DePeu's address is quite insightful and interesting, and is worth reading in its entirety. (See Bibliography)

Chapter 1

WHAT MAKES A MONUMENT A BILLBOARD MONUMENT?

*T*he short answer to this chapter's title question is "airspace"! But, there's more to it than that, so I begin by offering a little background. I spent many a fine day in 2014 surveying cemeteries in southern Maine while searching for markers created by the Bartlett Adams shop carvers. While visiting the Congregational Cemetery in Cumberland Center I found about a dozen that fit the bill. But I also noticed three large and interesting grave markers that I recorded in my field notes as "looks like a billboard." They consisted of long slabs—one slate, two marble—inscribed lengthwise and held above the ground. Two were on granite posts and one had a metal frame, but what they had in common was the airspace between the stone and the ground (and that they just look like billboards!).

After my book about Adams was published, Leslie Rounds, executive director of the Dyer Library/Saco Museum, invited me to wander with her through Saco's Laurel Hill Cemetery. She wanted to document all of the markers made in the Adams shop for her 2018 book about the cemetery (see Bibliography). We did find markers from the Adams shop, but also marveled at two large monuments held aloft on granite posts. I told Leslie I'd seen others like them in Cumberland and

The Paul family billboard, found at Laurel Hill Cemetery in Saco.

called them "billboards" for their similarity to the familiar highway signs. I was delighted to see she included one of them in her book, also referring to it as a billboard monument. From then on, the name stuck.

Early in 2019, I sought the help of MOCA (the Maine Old Cemetery Association) and the Northeast New England chapter of the AGS (the Association for Gravestone Studies) to document as many of these monuments in Maine as possible. With their enthusiastic help, 15 billboards were added to the list. I spent many hours that summer visiting each one, measuring and photographing them to aid in my research back home. As the collection grew, I began to refer to them as "family billboard" monuments, since it seemed more often than not that these stones memorialized multiple members of a family.

Billboards are quite rare; only 38 have been identified to date in Maine. They're found in ten counties and are spread over a distance of about 200 miles: as far south as York (York County), as far north as Dover-Foxcroft (Piscataquis County), and as far east as Bucksport (Hancock County). Massive, yet fragile, 60 percent of them have structural problems, from stress cracks to full breaks. It's no surprise that these are in peril given the very nature of their construction: heavy pieces of stone held up in the air—for decades!

English Roots

Having completed my field research, I took a deep dive into learning as much as possible about each of the 38 billboards and the people they memorialize. I built family trees, searched for interesting stories in newspapers and family genealogies, sorted through the similarities and differences in materials and construction, plotted them on a map (see Appendix), and documented the physical health of each. Questions regarding the origin of the design kept crossing my mind. Who came up with the idea of the billboard? When were they made? Was there just one maker? Are they found anywhere else? To answer those questions, I looked for clues in the work of others who have studied gravestones before me.

In his interesting 1963 book, *English Churchyard Memorials,* Frederick Burgess described seventeenth-century wooden grave markers, known as "grave-rails," which resembled a section of one of our common, modern-day post-and-rail fences. A grave-rail was a wooden rail fixed between two upright posts, generally running lengthwise down the grave. Such a narrow rail would not have allowed its maker to paint on much more than the name and date of the deceased. Burgess also described the "dead-board" or "grave-board," which consisted of a long wooden panel held aloft between decorated supporting posts. Also usually oriented lengthwise along the grave, grave-boards had more surface area than rails, better accommodating their painted inscriptions. He wrote that these types of wooden markers were commonly used in England as far back as the sixteenth century. He also noted that in some churchyards of Sussex County (due south of London, on the English Channel), wooden grave-boards from the 1700s were known to be constructed with supporting posts made of stone.

In 1968, researcher Benno M. Forman made the link between England and New England. He suggested that the reason why stone

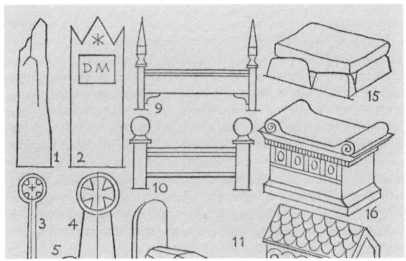

Detail from the Burgess book, 1963. Note numbers 9 and 10 in the center—elevated wooden panels he referred to as "dead-boards" or "grave-boards."

grave markers were rarely found in Massachusetts's Essex County[2] in the seventeenth century was because the settlers, largely from southern England where grave-rails and grave-boards had been in use, marked graves with what was familiar to them from their home country. Over time, the wooden monuments created in New England had completely deteriorated. The few stone markers that had been placed during the period simply better survived, leaving all of us with the false impression that they were the earliest forms.

In 1975, researcher Peter Benes investigated this subject further, building on Forman's work and suggesting that wooden grave markers were used throughout Massachusetts Bay Colony, not just in Essex County. He found probate files from the 1600s that detailed expenses for "coffins and rails." Those records showed a single payment to a woodworker who supplied both the coffin and the rail rather than separate payments to a coffin-maker and a stonecutter. New England rails were likely oriented similar to their English counterparts, running along the side of the grave. Benes also wrote that while no wooden

---

2. Essex County is in the northeast of Massachusetts, encompassing Salem, Gloucester, and Newburyport.

monuments were known to have survived in Massachusetts, there were some extant wooden grave-boards from the 1700s in South Carolina.

In 1990, researchers Elizabeth A. Crowell and Norman V. Mackie III published a paper regarding monument types of the colonial Tidewater Virginia region. While they did not have examples of grave-boards or other wooden markers in Virginia, they noted three from around 1775 that were known to have survived in South Carolina.

A colonial South Carolina wooden marker, circa 1775. Source: Crowell and Mackie.

More recently, in 2016, British gravestone scholar Jonathan Kewley published an article in the journal *Markers* in which he quite convincingly argues that the American colonists, not the English, were behind the design of the classic early slate markers found in the New World.[3] His article also briefly discusses the common use of wooden grave-rails and grave-boards in Britain through the eighteenth century

---

3. In this work, Kewley addresses those slate markers with the rounded top flanked by a pair of smaller rounded shoulders often called "bedsteads." They are commonly found in colonial New England cemeteries and dated from the late 1600s to the late 1700s.

and includes a picture of an extant grave-board located in Ardingly, Sussex, England. The painted inscription no longer survives, but the photo shows us a fine example of an English wooden grave-board.

Fig. 15. Wooden graveboard, Ardingly, Sussex.

An English wooden grave-board. Source: Kewley.

Jonathan also told me that one of the original grave-boards referenced by Crowell and Mackie, located in Charleston, South Carolina, was destroyed by Hurricane Hugo in 1989. A reproduction has been put in its place at St. Michael's Church Cemetery.

MAINE ROOTS

Today I have no reason to believe that the English settlers of Maine didn't also mark graves with materials and forms that were familiar to them from their homeland. Of course, given the passing of a few centuries and the relatively harsh Maine winter climate, it's logical to assume that any wooden markers they'd placed in the 1600s and 1700s simply haven't survived.

Stone obviously is better able to last through the ages. And while none of the 38 Maine billboards were made before the 1840s, there were other fairly common monuments used to memorialize families. Obelisks and columns found on family lots often hold inscriptions for an entire family. But the ledger, consisting of a large stone slab perhaps six feet by three feet, is worth mentioning. In Maine cemeteries, older ledgers are found in both slate and marble; newer ones are granite.

Sometimes they are found placed flat on the ground and therefore serve as a tomb cover; others are elevated off the ground and rest atop table tombs and box (or chest) tombs. These slabs work well for families, since there is plenty of space for the inscription of multiple names and dates. Inscriptions are found running from the top to the bottom of the long narrow slab (such as in the case of nearly all other grave markers that are predominantly taller than they are wide). But if we were to stand the slab upright, turn it 90 degrees (so that it is six feet *wide* and three feet *tall*), and attach it to granite posts to keep it elevated, we'd have a billboard!

Though badly broken, this ledger slab serves as a tomb cover and shows inscriptions running vertically. Billboards are inscribed horizontally.

The Maine billboards differ from the early wooden markers found in English cemeteries in another way. The majority—if not all—of Maine billboards are oriented as headstones on family lots. That is, they do not run lengthwise down the grave but instead serve as more typical tablet markers do in marking the head of the family lot. There are a couple of billboards on family lots that are set off enough from surrounding headstones to raise the question of their having an orientation running lengthwise, but if true, they are clearly exceptions to the majority.

"POCKET-SLOT" GRANITE POSTS

More than 30 of the Maine billboards use granite posts as the means to elevate the stone. Three have stones attached to posts with metal hooks and two have stones pinned to their posts, but the majority are fitted into slots cut into the posts themselves.

I further break down the slotted-post billboards into two categories. First is the "pocket-slot," where the stone fits snugly into the post's slots, giving the appearance of a pocket door. I imagine these would have been the more difficult to erect at the cemetery, since workers would have needed to either put the stone and posts together on the ground and then lift the whole monument up into place or put the posts in the ground, then splay them in order to fit the stone into the slots. Either option seems challenging when dealing with a marble slab weighing hundreds of pounds. In any case, there are 15 pocket-slot billboards in the Maine collection.

The Lane family billboard, located at Buxton's South Buxton (sometimes called Tory Hill) Cemetery, provides our first example. Note its construction, with the slots cut into the posts exactly the same length as the inscribed stone's height. This marble slab is just under four feet

The Lane billboard at South Buxton Cemetery is a pocket-slot post monument.

wide and has a dry weight of about 140 pounds.[4] Oddly, only two members of the family were memorialized on the monument: Jabez Lane's daughter Abigail and his wife, Elizabeth.[5] Town records list 11 children born to Jabez and Elizabeth Lane

---

4. I use the Amlink Marble Company's Material Weight Calculator to determine dry weight of the billboard monuments. After a good rain, stone (especially marble) absorbs moisture and can add 20 percent more weight to the monument.

5. Note two spelling errors on the monument. "Jabes" and "Elisabeth" were carved, but town records use the more traditional spelling of Jabez and refer to his wife using Elizabeth.

between 1794 and 1812, three of whom died well before Abigail did in 1837. In fact, Jabez himself died in 1836, between Elizabeth (who died 1834) and Abigail (1837). Why he and the other children who had predeceased him were excluded isn't clear.

"Drop-slot" Granite Posts

The second category of slotted-post billboards is the "drop-slot," where the slots extend to the top of the posts. This would have allowed the workers placing the monument to plant the posts in the ground at the correct distance from each other and then drop the stone down into place. It's interesting to note that some of the drop-slot billboards were designed such that the height of the slots matches exactly with the height of the stone, so that the stone fits perfectly into the whole monument; others have much shorter slots, so the stone dropped into place has a finished appearance that lifts it far above the tops of the posts. There are a dozen drop-slot billboards in the Maine collection.

The Leavitt family billboard at the Plains Cemetery in Auburn provides our example. This stone memorializes five—father, mother, and three of their children—on a marble slab that is a bit more square than most of the others. Martin and Julia Ann (Hotchkiss) Leavitt married in 1815, had 11 children over a 20-year span, and lived long enough to celebrate their 56th anniversary in Auburn in 1871.[6] The marble billboard is just under three feet wide by

The Leavitt billboard at Auburn's Plains Cemetery is a drop-slot post monument.

---

6. Their celebration was covered in the *Portland Daily Press* newspaper on December 18, 1871.

Detail of the Leavitt billboard, showing how the slab fits into its posts.

two feet tall and, like the Lane monument above, has a dry weight of 140 pounds. It's located at the front of Auburn's Plains Cemetery, facing busy Route 4. Drivers zipping northward on that road might glance to their right and assume the monument is actually a sign for the cemetery itself.

Driving along Route 4 in Auburn, it's easy to mistake this billboard monument for a cemetery signboard.

CHAPTER 2

INSCRIBED ON BOTH SIDES

*B*illboard monuments worked well for large families; their large slabs have plenty of room for inscriptions. Most billboards were created without decorative elements and instead just contained the information about lost loved ones. When only one side is inscribed, that is, of course, the front. For the few that are inscribed on both sides, we can determine which is the front by looking at the direction it faces on the lot, by how it compares to other nearby markers in the cemetery, or by who is memorialized on each side. Two double-sided billboards are featured in this chapter; the third is covered in Chapter 3.

THE PAUL FAMILY MONUMENT, SACO

The first example is from Laurel Hill Cemetery. It's the Paul family billboard, a pocket-slot type that's made of marble. The stone is just under six feet long and has a dry weight of about 275 pounds. Note that the monument has a full break in one corner that puts it in some jeopardy of completely falling from its granite posts.

Eight members of the Paul family are memorialized, including the family's patriarch, Joshua. He was born in 1797 and married

The front side of the Paul family billboard in Saco.

Jane Robinson Macomber of Effingham, New Hampshire, in 1827. The couple had at least ten children between 1828 and 1844. Joshua worked in a cotton mill as a dyer and died in 1857 at the age of 60. In addition to Joshua Paul, four of his sons, two of his daughters, and one granddaughter join him on the monument's list of names.

As is the case with most billboards, the carver etched vertical lines on the stone to create multiple inscription panels. The Paul monument has three panels on each side; the spacing of the lettering allowed for the inclusion of up to 12 members of the family. I date the billboard to the 1850s, given the inscriptions found. Assuming that the family's patriarch would be inscribed on the front side, the first panel on the front names Joshua's sons Loring M. (died 1852, age 20) and William F. (died 1833, age 3). The center panel names another son, Otis S. (who died a month after Loring in 1852, age 24), and Otis's three-month-old daughter, Eleanor J., who died in 1851. Joshua is alone on the third panel. Space below him was left open, no doubt intended for his wife, Jane. But her name does not appear on the billboard. Jane apparently didn't remarry and outlived Joshua by at least 13 years. She appeared in the 1860 and 1870 Saco census records as "head of household" (at age 60 and 70, respectively). In 1860 she had five children living with

18

her, from age 15 to age 27, but by 1870 at least two had died and the only child living with her was her daughter Susan, who was working in a straw hat shop. Jane isn't found in the 1880 census, nor could I find vital records of her death or burial.

The back side of the Paul family billboard. Only one panel has been inscribed. The crack in the slab is evident.

On the reverse side of this billboard there's an empty first panel, then the center panel lists two of Joshua and Jane's unmarried adult daughters, Carrie M. (died 1858, age 21) and Rachel M. (died 1864, age 20). The third panel names son Silas M. (died 1862, age 19). During research of the family for her book, Leslie Rounds found vital records that revealed that consumption had taken at least four of them. Another died of typhoid pneumonia.

THE PETTINGILL FAMILY MONUMENT, LIVERMORE FALLS

A pleasant little hilltop cemetery in Livermore Falls that's surrounded on three sides by mixed woods holds the billboard monument of the Pettingill family. But for the sign placed close to Route 133, it would be easy to miss the Shuy Yard Cemetery. The listing on the Find-a-Grave website includes just 22 known burials, but when I visited I noticed that a survey must have been recently done, as a few metal discs mark additional plots that are otherwise undecorated with gravestones.

Elisha H. Pettingill was born in 1819. He married Rosanah Bean in 1841, and within a few years they had two children, Mary and Elbridge. Sadly, within a three-week period in 1848, Rosanah and the

The front side of the Pettingill family billboard in Livermore Falls.

Note the interesting background design and lettering on the Pettingill monument.

two children died. Elisha was just turning 30 when he lost his entire family; his wife was 24 and the children were just 1 and 5.

The billboard's front side, facing the road, was designed with a simple frame around the inscriptions. The lettering used for the three names is quite beautifully done on a background patterned with etched swirls. The back side was left without any framing or other decoration and, like most, was probably never intended to be used. This monument, at five feet long, appears to have been erected by a loving husband and father to honor the memory of his young family. Under the inscriptions for the two children, we find this verse:

> Friends and physicians could not save
> Their mortal bodies from the grave
> Nor can the grave confine them hear (sic)
> When Christ shall call them to appear

Elisha quickly moved on with his life, remarrying within a year of losing his family. He and his second wife, Sarah, had two children, a son in 1850 they named Elbridge Wilson and a daughter in 1852 they named Sarah Jane. Census records for the next three decades show that Elisha was a farmer and Sarah was keeping house. Both of their children reached adulthood. In 1884, Cyrus Knapp was appointed by the Androscoggin County Court to represent Elisha, who was then considered "a person of unsound mind." Around the same time, Sarah died. In 1900, Elisha was 80 and living with his son Elbridge and his family. Six years later, Elisha died, his cause of death on the vital record being "senile debility."

The reverse side of the Pettingill family billboard; Elisha's name was inscribed at top center.

Rather than erecting a new stone for his father, it appears that Elbridge instead had Elisha's name inscribed on the reverse side of the same monument that Elisha had erected for his own family more than 50 years earlier. In simple block letters, centered on the back of the billboard, we find:

Elisha H. Pettingill
Died Jan. 21, 1906
AE. 86.

CHAPTER 3

THE WRECK OF THE *ISIDORE* IN 1842

*T*he third billboard inscribed on both sides is found on North Street in Kennebunkport at a burial ground that's had multiple names over the years, including The Tombs, Kennebunkport Cemetery, Village Cemetery, and Bass Cove Cemetery. There's no sign at the

The front side of the Foss-Goodwin family billboard in Kennebunkport.

entrance, but the latter two names seem to be the most commonly used today, so I've chosen to use Bass Cove in my notes simply for its more descriptive name.

The billboard memorializes six members of the Foss family, three members of the Goodwin family, and a woman whose relationship to them remains a mystery. The Foss and Goodwin families are well connected as we'll see, but the starting point for this chapter comes from the *Christian Mirror* newspaper of December 8, 1842.

> *Loss of the ship Isadora, with all her crew.*
>
> "KENNEBUNK, Dec. 1, 1842.
> The new ship Isadora, built at this place, bound to New Orleans, which sailed yesterday noon, before the commencement of the storm, was wrecked in the course of the night, and Captain Foss and the whole crew perished—fifteen in number. She was wrecked a little to the eastward of Bald Head and the ship went entirely to peices. Capt. Silas Grant, of Kennebunkport, was a passenger on board and is also lost. The whole crew were of this port and probably all lost, within eight or ten hours from the time the vessel left the wharf. The ship had a fine crew nearly all experienced seamen and of respectable families; most of them had wives and children at home, and all left friends by whom they were held dear."
>
> The names of those on board were, Leander Foss, master; Clement Stone, 1st mate; John Crowder, 2d mate; Paul M Grant, John Tendell, George Lewis, George Davis, Wm. Harding, James Murphy, Charles Lord, George F. Hutchins, James Young, Mr. Thompson, Alvin Huff, Daniel Perkins, all of Kennebunkport. Five of the above had families, and have left 20 children; two were the only sons of their mothers who were widows.—*Am.*

Article from the Christian Mirror, *December 8, 1842.*

CAPTAIN LEANDER FOSS (1806–1842)

Leander Foss was born in 1806. He was a sea captain when he married Maria A. Smithen about 1832; they had four children over a ten-year period. Youngest daughter Lavinia Margarita Foss was born in April of 1842, just seven months before her father died. He, along with 14 others, was lost in a stormy sea ten miles south of their home that November. Captain Foss was not among the seven whose bodies were recovered and buried in area graveyards after the storm. The marble billboard that was erected for this family is one of the largest found: at over six feet wide and nearly three feet tall, it weighs over 400 pounds. There's a large fracture line in the upper-right panel, though for now the stone seems to be holding securely in place. The center panel on

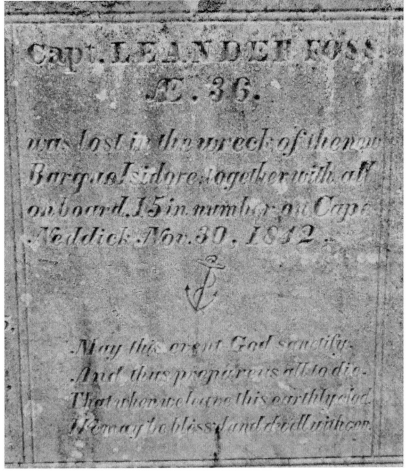

The center front panel of the Foss-Goodwin billboard, dedicated to Capt. Leander Foss.

the front side is dedicated to the memory of the captain, whose death left his young wife a widow and his four young children fatherless.

The *Isidore* was built in Kennebunk for Captain Foss. It was on its maiden voyage, destination New Orleans, when it went down in a nor'easter that had hit the southern Maine coastline quite quickly and severely but lasted just a few hours. The storm left behind up to a foot of snow, wind damage, and, of course, too many lives lost. In the aftermath of the storm, the immediate shoreline at the site of the wreck was littered with broken pieces of the ship and unidentifiable battered body parts of the 15 men who had perished. In all, at least 20 children were left fatherless. A year later, a writer for *The Sailor's Magazine and Naval Journal* reflected on the distressing wreck of the *Isidore*, noting, "A fatal shipwreck strikes a blow which is felt far and wide. It is not the immediate victims alone who are the sufferers. It inflicts a long and wasting agony on mothers and sisters, and other kindred."

CHARLES W. GOODWIN (1804–1871)

Two years before Leander Foss was born, Charles W. Goodwin had been born in Kennebunkport. He became a sailmaker and certainly would have known Captain Foss; in fact, Goodwin could very well have supplied Foss with sails for the *Isidore*. Charles married Mary Pope about 1829 and together they had seven children over ten years. With the tragic loss of the *Isidore* in 1842, we can imagine that the Goodwin family offered whatever comfort and support they could to the Foss family living nearby. Charles experienced his own loss just two years later, when in 1844 his wife, Mary, died at the age of 38. Less than a year after Mary's death the two families were united when Charles W. Goodwin, a widower with six young children in his household, married Maria S. Foss, a widow who brought her own four children into their new blended family.

The 1850 census for Kennebunkport shows this large family headed by Charles Goodwin, a sailmaker who was then 46 years old. In the household were Maria (age 37), five children named Goodwin ranging from age 12 to 17, and four children named Foss ranging from 7 to 17.

In the 1860 census, Charles was still working as a sailmaker, though he also had a position with the town. According to a February 1860 newspaper, he was "Coroner of Wrecks and Lost Goods for Kennebunkport," which I imagine involved the investigation into and documentation of cargo lost as the result of shipwrecks along the local coast (and a role he may have played earlier following the wreck of the *Isidore*). Charles was head of a shrinking household. Only three kids still lived with him and Maria, one from his first marriage and two from hers.

MORE TRAGEDY: A FIRE

In April of 1867, a fire was discovered in a Kennebunkport store near the Goodwin home. According to the newspaper account of this incident, the fire spread very quickly and "necessitated pulling down the house of Mr. Charles Goodwin to save the dwelling of Captain Robert Towne." Apparently the sacrifice worked and the Towne home was untouched by the fire. But, the story continued, "Mr. Goodwin loses a good house, connected by an L to his barn, and also suffers some loss of furniture." There was no insurance on the buildings or goods owned by Charles Goodwin.

HENRY B. FOSS (1833–1872)

The eldest child of Captain Leander and Maria, Henry B. Foss was a 26-year-old sailmaker who had moved out of the Foss family home in 1860. In fact, he had just gotten married to Eliza Gooch, age 24, a couple of months before the 1860 census was recorded. The newlyweds shared their home with Henry's younger brother Leander Foss Jr., a tailor, and his wife, Phebe, and they all lived just two doors away from Charles and Maria Goodwin.

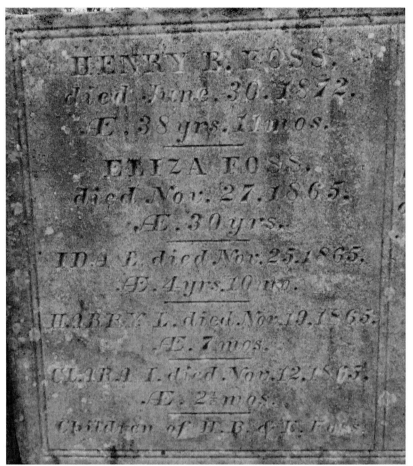

Detail of the panel for Henry Foss's family.

In 1865, over a ten-day period in November, Henry experienced his own tragic loss. His two children and wife, Eliza, died of diphtheria. This sad situation was covered in at least three Maine newspapers during the time that Eliza was still ill. In one, the final line written in regard to Eliza was, "Should she die, Mr. Foss will have lost his whole family." In fact, within a couple of days Eliza did die and indeed Henry Foss lost his whole family.

The billboard monument found at the Foss family graves was most likely erected after Henry's death in 1872. His name appears at the top of the first inscription panel on the front side. Just underneath

> Mr. Henry B. Foss, of Kennebunkport, has during the past week, lost by death from diptheria, his two children, and his wife is very sick with the same disease with but slight hope of her recovery.—*Saco Democrat.*

One of the newspaper articles published shortly before Eliza's death.

are the names and dates of his wife and two children who had died together six years earlier, plus an infant daughter who had predeceased them in 1862 or 1863.[7] The third panel on the front side has just one inscription:

MARGARET BARTLETT
died Mar. 29, 1855
AE. 82 years

There's no information that names her as "mother of…" or some other relationship to the Foss family. No clear vital or census records are found for her. The only clue to her identity comes from her death notice in the newspaper, which simply noted that she was a widow. In 2016, Priscilla Eaton published an interesting article in *The Maine Genealogist* (see Bibliography), in which she provided detailed genealogical information for all 15 men lost in the wreck of the *Isidore*. She mentioned the mystery of Margaret Bartlett's identity as well, but wondered if *Margaret* might have been grandmother to Lavinia *Margarita* Foss (the last of Captain Leander's children, born a few months before

---

7. It appears the stone-carver erred on using 1865 as the year of Clara's death. The more likely date was 1862 or 1863. Clara had already predeceased the others, as she was not mentioned in the 1865 newspaper articles about the family.

he was lost at sea). Leander's mother was named *Lavinia*, so it's possible that this child was named for both of her grandmothers.[8]

The Goodwins of this blended family occupy the reverse side of the Foss-Goodwin billboard monument. Only the center panel is inscribed. At the top is Mary Pope, first wife of Charles Goodwin, who had died in 1844. The names of Charles and his second wife, Maria A. Foss Goodwin, are inscribed below hers. They both died in their sixties in the 1870s.

Over the years many facts have been gathered—and many tales have been spun—about the wreck of the *Isidore*. For those wishing to explore the event further, a trip to the Kennebunkport Historical Society is recommended. For the genealogical information about the 15 lost souls and details about the burial locations of the seven bodies that were recovered, see Priscilla Eaton's work. For a book (and original music) dedicated to this tragedy, see Harvey Reid's work. The billboard monument itself is a fine memorial to the ship's captain and family, and is certainly worth visiting to pay our respects to them.

The Wreck.

Photo of the wreck of the Isidore. *Source: Brooks.*

8. Lavinia Margarita's mother, Maria, was named Smither or Smithen, from New York, but records are a challenge in her regard. It is possible that her mother was named Margaret and that she was either born a Bartlett or remarried into that name.

CHAPTER 4

TWENTY CHILDREN

Some Maine parents used family billboards only to memorialize their children. The marble slabs of the five monuments described in this chapter are fully inscribed; the fact that none have empty panels suggests that the billboards were erected specifically for those children rather than intended for use over time for the entire family as we saw with the Pauls of Saco in Chapter 2.

Dates of death for this chapter's 20 children range from 1830 to 1875; the age range is two months to 22 years. Few "cause of death" vital records were found, so I looked to other sources to understand likely causes. Of course, these midcentury families didn't have the benefit of today's trained medical professionals or advanced medical treatments. Few understood the transmission causes of deadly bacterial illnesses such as cholera or viral infections such as influenza. Once those conditions took hold of a family, there was often a devastating loss of life.

In 1866, the US government released a state-by-state report on mortality for the year ending June 1, 1860. Consumption, a highly contagious bacterial infection better known as TB or tuberculosis, was by far the greatest cause of death in Maine, accounting for 30 percent of all deaths, or 2,169 people. In fact, of the 40 states and territories included in the report,[9] Maine had the highest ratio of deaths due to consumption. Another bacterial infection, typhoid fever, was the second-greatest cause of death (434 people, or 6 percent), followed by "scarlatina" (yet another bacterial infection, now called scarlet fever) at 4 percent. Since antibiotic medicines were not yet in use, it's no surprise that these bacterial illnesses were so prevalent and so deadly. That report also showed that 25 percent of all deaths in Maine were for children under age five; 40 percent of all deaths in the state were for people under the age of 20.

In 1869, the Maine Medical Association published a report of the epidemics known in Maine in 1866. Sixty physicians were surveyed throughout the state and reported local outbreaks of influenza, typhoid pneumonia, jaundice (non-fatal), typhoid fever, whooping cough, and dysentery, among others. Smallpox, cholera, and yellow fever epidemics were recorded throughout the United States in the midcentury as well, though they were not predominant killers in the 1850s and 1860s in Maine.[10]

THE HOUSTON FAMILY MONUMENT, DOVER-FOXCROFT

Records for Joseph and Loritta (Spaulding) Houston are not perfect, but the couple appears to have had 12 kids over a 25-year period. Four of them died in the 1830s, and the billboard erected in their honor is found near the top of a long downward slope at Dover Cemetery. Loritta Houston has her own marker adjacent to her children's billboard; she passed in 1843.

Four of the Houstons' daughters are on this monument, and the order of the placement of their names does not follow the order in which they were born or died; instead they're listed according to their

---

9. In 1860 there were 33 states, six territories, and the District of Columbia.

10. Smallpox was troublesome for decades throughout the 1700s and 1800s. Yellow fever, a mosquito-borne disease, affected the southern US more than the North, though some cases were reported for Maine.

ages at the times of their deaths, from youngest to oldest. Emeline died at age two months, Helen at nine months, Sybil at 12 years, and Joann at 22 years. Running along the bottom of the marble slab we find inscribed, "Children of Joseph & Loritta Houston."

This billboard was most likely created closer to the middle of the

The Houston family billboard at Dover Cemetery.

century and backdated to the 1830s. Its design is very similar to others from the 1850s and 1860s. Note especially how each name is carved within its own banner, a style very commonly found on markers later in the century. This monument is of the drop-slot granite post variety, but the stone rests very high above the posts themselves, given the short length of the slots carved into the posts (compare this to the Foss-Goodwin monument in the last chapter, which rests all the way down into the posts).

THE MUDGETT FAMILY MONUMENT, PROSPECT

The Mudgett family monument at Maple Grove Cemetery in Prospect is quite similar in size and design to the Houston marker. Running along the bottom of the marble slab we find "Children of Nehemiah & Mary Jane Mudgett." It memorializes four of the family's nine children, who passed between 1840 and 1852. These kids were listed chronologically by year of death. Nehemiah was a shoemaker and lived in Prospect for most of his life, but moved to nearby Belfast by 1880. Some siblings of the four named on the billboard died in later years and were buried in Belfast.

The Mudgett family billboard in Prospect.

THE HILL FAMILY MONUMENT, WELLS

The third monument, similar again in size and style to the Houston and Mudgett billboards, is found at the Ocean View Cemetery in Wells. Like the other two, it holds a line at the bottom of the slab which notes these are the "Children of Captain Charles & Sarah W. Hill." Though located 150 miles southwest of the other two, I suspect these three markers were created by the same maker.

Captain Charles Hill was born 1806 and his first wife, Mary Deane, 1808. They had at least two children before Mary died in 1845 at the

The Hill family billboard in Wells.

age of 37. Captain Hill remarried the next year, to Sarah Winn (born 1815). They had at least five more children together. The four memorialized on the billboard were all Sarah's children. Mary D. Hill is listed first with a death date of July 7, 1849; no age is given for her, so I suspect she may have died the same day she was born. The other three children died within a month of each other in the fall of 1852; James was 4, Myron 2, and Leroy 5.

The billboard was likely erected soon after 1852. The Hills have a large elevated family lot set off by coping stones near a brick building at the center of the cemetery. Immediately next to the children's billboard is a tall marble column that was erected for the captain when he died in 1867 at age 61. Below his name on the column we find

The family lot at Ocean View Cemetery in Wells, showing the Hill billboard and column monuments.

The column includes the names of the four children also listed on the billboard.

his two wives, Mary D. (died 1845) and Sarah W. (died 1889). Another panel on the column is dedicated to the four children already listed on the billboard. A third panel has the inscription of Charles A. Hill, who was Mary's son. A mariner like his father, he died at sea in March of 1866 at the age of 26.

As I worked on the family tree for the Hills, the name of Sarah Winn Hill's mother stood out: Philadelphia A. (Maxwell) Winn. Philadelphia's parents have their own billboard monument in Ogunquit and are featured in Chapter 15. This means that the four Hill children on the Wells billboard are the great-great-grandchildren of Philadelphia Maxwell of Ogunquit.

THE ELDEN FAMILY MONUMENT, BUXTON

Found at the South Buxton (or Tory Hill) Cemetery, the Elden billboard is unusual for its decoration: there are rosebuds carved above each of the three children's names. It also has the thickest-cut marble slab of all 38 billboards known in Maine. At 41 inches wide, it is among the smaller of the billboards with respect to inscribable surface area, but at four inches thick—double the thickness of most others—the stone has a dry weight of 265 pounds. Note also the metal bar that runs just underneath the stone. About half of all bill-

The Elden family billboard at South Buxton Cemetery.

boards have such a bar, intended to help keep the two posts upright and minimize the possibility that the weight of the stone (and gravity) would push the posts apart.

William and Sarah Elden married in Buxton in 1848 and had eight children over an 18-year period. Between August 12 and September 11, 1875, three of them died. Charley was 5, Emma was 7, and Annie was 10. I asked Jan Hill, president of the Buxton-Hollis Historical Society, whether she had records of any epidemics in the area in the fall of 1875. She said that there were waves of influenza around the 1873 to 1875 period, adding "Given the practices and hygiene of the period—including kids in the 17 one-room schools sharing the same water buckets and ladles during the school day—it is not surprising that germs were quickly shared."

When William and Sarah died many years after their three children, they were buried at the same cemetery with their own markers.

THE TRAFTON FAMILY MONUMENT, YORK

The final example in this chapter memorializes five children of Benjamin and Julia Ann (Young) Trafton, who were buried at the First Parish Cemetery in York. Perhaps more than any of the other chil-

The Trafton family billboard in York.

dren's billboards, the Trafton monument reflects the tragic loss related to medical illnesses endured by families in the nineteenth century. Within just two weeks in May of 1863, the Traftons lost five of their six children. Four boys and one girl, aged 2 through 11, died between May 14 and May 31 that year. Though no vital records provide cause of death details, surely what took them down was a dangerous and highly communicable disease. Only seven-year-old Benjamin Jr. survived; he became a carpenter, married twice, and had at least eight children of his own. He died in 1932.

After their devastating loss, Benjamin and Julia Ann had at least seven more children between 1863 and 1877. The couple was buried at the First Parish Cemetery with their own markers, Benjamin in 1897 (age 72) and Julia Ann in 1917 (age 84).

Today the marble billboard is easy to find. It is five feet long and so bright white, it really stands out. The stone has two full breaks on the left side that caused it to completely fall from its posts. The good news is that the marker is back up in the air, thanks to someone who has

Detail of repairs made to the Trafton billboard.

reconnected the two smaller broken pieces to the large right side of the slab. The bad news is that the substance used to reconnect the pieces is not what I would expect a professional conservator to use today. The jet-black material appears to be somewhat pliable and reminds me of the compound one uses to seal cracks in a paved driveway. Had the billboard's cracks been repaired professionally using a color-correct mortar, the fracture lines would practically disappear from view.

Like many marble monuments created 150-plus years ago, this billboard is heavily eroded. Four-line verses are inscribed in the lower left and right corners. The left side I am just unable to read; on the right side I'm able to get most of the words, and certainly the sentiment:

> Our little ____(?) have gone
> To rest in Heaven above
> We know they are not alone
> They dwell with God in love.

CHAPTER 5

ARRESTED AND IMPRISONED

*T*he largest billboard in the Maine collection memorializes Cyrus Foss Sargent and family. It's found at the Hillside (also known as Old Baptist) Cemetery in Yarmouth. At seven feet wide and over two feet tall, the marble monument has a dry weight of 450 pounds (when soaked with rainwater, it's likely 500). Though the granite posts are also massive and appear sound, the slab itself has three visible two-inch stress cracks running along the lower edge; I worry that the monument is in jeopardy of having one of the cracks grow into a full break.

The Sargent billboard at Hillside Cemetery, Yarmouth.

Dated 1853

This is one of just two billboards that are dated. The Sargent billboard has three inscription panels and a top edge that has an attractive scalloped design. The center panel holds the patriarch's details and is decorated with a freemason's compass and square, flanked by two urns. The urn on the left is inscribed with the word "Erected" and the one on the right has the date "1853."

Detail of the Sargent billboard. Note the word "Erected" and the date "1853" in the urns.

First Marriage, 1844: Mary Margaret Hill

Cyrus Foss Sargent was born in Yarmouth in 1814 and died in Yarmouth in 1880, but in between those dates he lived an eventful and interesting life filled with travel, success, sorrow, and even a short stay in prison. He married three times. His first wife was Mary Margaret Hill, born 1826 and memorialized on the billboard. In fact, Mr. Sargent probably had the monument erected for her; she died at age 26 in the summer of 1852 in Champagnolle, Arkansas. A close look at the left-hand panel of the billboard reveals more details. At the bottom of the marker we find "Remains removed 1853," which, of course, is the same date found in the urns flanking Cyrus Sargent's name. Embalming had not yet been perfected and was not in common use when Mary died. We don't know the exact details of the transfer of Mary's remains, but a likely option was that her body was preserved in spirits. The Yarmouth Historical Society has record of such a transfer of remains of another person to Yarmouth in this period. In any event, this wasn't the first time Cyrus Sargent had moved the remains of a family member back home to Yarmouth.

Cyrus and Mary had four children. When Mary died in 1852, only two were still living, Grace (born 1849) and Cyrus (born 1852). Daughter Lucy Elinor had died in Yarmouth just a few months after her birth in 1848. But her five-year-old sister Alice Mary died in New Orleans in 1850. The girls share the right-hand panel on this marker. Underneath Alice's name we find "Alice's remains removed 1850."

Detail of the Sargent billboard. Note the line at the bottom regarding removal of Alice's remains.

Ties to Louisiana and Arkansas

Cyrus Sargent had carved out a very successful business that brought him frequently from Maine to New Orleans and Arkansas. Author Michael J. Connolly wrote that Sargent had been working as a merchant in New Orleans as early as the 1830s and then as a land speculator in Arkansas by the 1840s, while maintaining Yarmouth as his primary home. Author John A. Marshall agreed, writing that Sargent spent two or three years in New Orleans when he was just 19 (that is, around 1833 to 1835) before moving to Arkansas. Marshall noted that Sargent acquired "quite a fortune" there, given that Arkansas was then in a "prosperous and flourishing condition." His marriage to Mary Hill and the birth of his first four children occurred during this period. The 1850 census for Arkansas included Cyrus Sargent as a merchant, age 35; in the household were his wife, Mary, (then 25) and daughters Alice and Grace, both of whom were born in Arkansas. Later that year, Alice died in New Orleans. In 1852, his son Cyrus Jr. was born in Arkansas and, of course, his wife, Mary, died there.

Cyrus and his two children—one age 4 and the other just an infant—returned to Maine in 1853, along with Mary's remains. Within a couple of years, he married for the second time.

Second Marriage, 1855: Olive Elizabeth Blanchard

Cyrus's second marriage occurred back home in Yarmouth and, like Mary before her, Olive delivered four children. In another parallel, two of Olive's children died in infancy; one other lived to age 12, and only Elizabeth Alice, born 1857, reached adulthood. Even she predeceased her father, though, as she died at the age of 22 soon after her marriage in 1877.

The 1860 census for Yarmouth included Cyrus at age 45, Olive at age 38, and four children: Grace (age 10) and Cyrus (8) from first wife, Mary, and Elizabeth (3) and Mary (2) from second wife, Olive.

Though primarily based in Yarmouth that year, Cyrus joined with his brother and two brothers-in-law from his first marriage (that is, Mary Hill's brothers) to form a New Orleans–based shipping company named Sargent & Hill. Connolly noted that this company had a "slave-holding interest." Family biographer Craig Stinson found records confirming that Sargent owned slaves. So, leading up to the Civil War, Cyrus Sargent was living in Maine among a majority of people opposed to the idea of slavery while enriching himself in the South from a business partnership with a labor force that included enslaved people. He had become a very wealthy man by 1860, with a net worth in today's dollars exceeding $1.5 million.[11]

1861 would prove to be a very challenging year for the family. There are records of an unnamed child who was born (probably stillborn) and died that year. This was likely coincident to Olive's death in April. All space on the 1853 billboard was already spoken for, so Olive was buried at Hillside Cemetery near the other members of the family with her own marker.

THE ARREST

The loss of his second wife in April 1861 left Cyrus Sargent a single parent of four children aged 3 to 11. Tension was high across the country; two weeks before Olive's death, Union soldiers had been attacked at Fort Sumter, South Carolina, setting the Civil War into motion. Cyrus was living in Maine, but his business interests were still primarily in the South. Given his standing in the community, he was asked to speak at an antiwar convention in Portland. During his address, he denounced the war but expressed sympathy for the southern cause. This did not settle well among some of the locals, and rumors began to circulate that Sargent was using his shipping business to run supplies to the South.

---

11. His 1860 combined estate value was reported by Connolly to be $63,200 (or about $1.5 million today).

It didn't take long for one of Yarmouth's preachers to become overly suspicious that Sargent's true allegiance was not with the Union. He sent a letter to the US secretary of state warning of Sargent's alleged activities and suggesting that he would soon likely head south to aid the Confederacy in its efforts. Sargent was arrested on his way to Boston, but whether he was leaving Maine to aid the South or simply to attend to his business isn't exactly clear.

The details of Cyrus Sargent's arrest are found in at least two sources. Connolly's account, published in 2012, cast no bias toward either the South or North. He wrote quite matter-of-factly, "...while riding the Portland to Boston train, US marshals jumped and handcuffed Sargent, brought him to Boston, and quickly put him on the New York City train. The next day he was incarcerated at Fort Lafayette, along with other political prisoners, and in late October shifted to Fort Warren in Boston harbor."

On the other hand, Marshall's account, published in *American Bastile* in 1874, clearly took the southern point of view (suggested by the very subtitle of his book, *A History of the Illegal Arrests and Imprisonment of American Citizens During the Late Civil War*). He wrote of the "brutal manner" in which Sargent was treated on September 23, 1861:

> While seated in a car reading the morning paper, he was attacked by four ruffians...One, a Deputy United States Marshal, came up behind him, and jumped upon him, crushing him down between the seats. The others got hold of him by the head and arms, three holding him, while a fourth handcuffed him.
>
> Immediately on being permitted to rise, he demanded their authority for thus acting, when the Deputy Marshal took from his pocket a paper, saying, "This is my authority." Mr. Sargent asked permission to read it, but was refused. He then requested the Marshal to do so, but this he also declined. After ironing him securely, they searched his person, when one of the four...drew his revolver, saying "This is the thing we settle such fellows as you with."

The Imprisonment

Marshall wrote that nobody aboard the train "had the manliness to raise his voice against the brutal manner in which the prisoner was treated." He noted that Sargent was allowed neither the opportunity to write a note home nor to attend to the "calls of nature." From Boston, Cyrus Sargent was transferred to New York, and placed in "a loathsome dungeon in the Tombs...compelled to pass the night amid a horrible stench." Sargent was transferred to Fort Hamilton (New York) on September 24. Marshall's account continues:

> He was placed in one of the casements, which was crowded with other victims of Puritanical tyranny. He was without a blanket or mattress for several nights, and suffered much from the cold while lying in the damp brick-floored casemate. He was unable to eat the scanty food furnished him.... The water, for the first ten days during his imprisonment, was filled with live, snakish-looking insects, and was so offensive that the prisoners had to close their nostrils while drinking it.

At the end of October, Cyrus Sargent was sent to Boston's Fort Warren, where—Marshall admitted—conditions were better. However, as to the transport ship, Marshall wrote, "The suffering of the prisoners, while on this rotten, unseaworthy steamer, beggars description. The hold was crowded with Hatteras prisoners, kept without food for forty-eight hours; and, on arriving at Fort Warren, some of them were nearly dead, and survived but a few days."

Back home in Yarmouth, family members and business associates were writing to the US attorney general asking for Sargent's release. The allegations against him—that he had a plan to supply the Confederacy, that he was building a ship to carry those supplies, that he had openly denounced the government, and that he avowed sympathy with treason—were easily debunked or explained by his supporters. He simply had a business in the South, they argued, he hadn't built a ship intending to supply the Confederacy after all, and nobody had really ever heard him denounce the government. The US attorney agreed the case was weak and ordered Cyrus Sargent's release, as long as Sargent would swear loyalty to the Union. Sargent did, and was released on November 10, 1861.

Cyrus Foss Sargent in later years. Source: Rowe. Photo courtesy of Craig Stinson.

THIRD MARRIAGE, 1867: HARRIET HAYES WRIGHT

Cyrus Sargent emerged from this ordeal and returned to Yarmouth, with four children to care for and his business interests to manage. In the 1866 Portland directory, "Cyrus F. Sargent & al." was listed as owner of two registered shipping vessels. One was the "Grace Sargent," built in 1859 and named for his daughter who was 10 years old at the time (she would live to 1878). Cyrus was married for the final time in 1867, to his neighbor Harriet Hayes Wright. He was 52; she was 42. She brought a son from her previous marriage into the family.

Though the Sargent billboard holds the names of four members of the family, at least ten in his direct line are buried at Hillside cemetery. In addition to Cyrus F. Sargent, who passed in 1880, two of his wives, six children, and one grandchild have markers there.

Chapter 6

BROTHERS & SISTERS, FATHER & MOTHER

*J*ust inside the gate at Yarmouth's Hillside Cemetery is the second of two billboards that are dated. This one, with a familial link to the Sargent billboard of Chapter 5, was erected in 1859 for the Hill family. Though heavy erosion has worn away some detail in the lettering and lichen has taken hold on the surface of the slab, a maker's signature can be detected in the lower right corner.

The monument is quite large at six feet long and about 400 pounds, but it is in rough shape. In addition to the surface issues just noted,

The Hill family billboard at Hillside Cemetery.

there is a full fracture between the second and third panels. A stone post has been retrofitted immediately underneath the crack to keep the slab level and prevent it from completely falling. The slotted granite posts appear to be sound. Hopefully, this monument will survive for years, but it is certainly threatened.

The top of each of the three panels is inscribed with a descriptive header to help the visitor know who is memorialized. The left panel's header is "Brothers & Sisters," the right panel reads "Father & Mother," and the center panel gives us the identity of the sibling and son of the ten people named on the monument. It reads, "Erected by J. C. Hill, Esq. 1859."

The center panel of the Hill monument contains the names of siblings of James and Mary Hill. Note date at the top: 1859.

JAMES COFFIN HILL (1792–1864)

Outlasting all eight siblings and both of his parents, James Coffin Hill of Yarmouth had this billboard monument placed in 1859. Death of family was familiar to him by then. He was the father of Mary Margaret Hill, first wife of Cyrus Sargent, both of whom are memorialized on the other billboard at Hillside Cemetery just discussed in the last chapter. In fact, the idea of placing a billboard for his siblings and parents very likely came from seeing the one his son-in-law Cyrus Sargent had erected for Mary in 1853. James worked in a variety of fields; various sources note that he was a lawyer, postmaster, merchant, and auctioneer. He was married to Mary B. Stockin (sometimes Stocking) in 1812 and they had seven children. His wife, Mary, and four of their children predeceased him. Mary passed in 1853 at the age of 63 (a year after his daughter Mary had passed). So by 1859, James had no doubt shed many tears for the 15 deaths in his direct family line. He was truly the last man standing. Five years after he had the billboard monument installed, James himself died at age 72. He and his wife Mary share a marker of their own nearer to the Sargent billboard than to the Hill billboard at the cemetery.

Craig Stinson is a modern-day descendent of this family; he lives in Arkansas and has written an excellent family genealogy entitled *A Brief History of Our Hill Family in America*. While conducting my research, Craig and I shared many emails about the Hill and Sargent families. My friend through the Association for Gravestone Studies, Abby Burnett, has researched the Hills in Arkansas and knows much of their Arkansas story. She loaned me her copy of Craig's book and introduced me to Teresa Harris, the historian for Ouachita County, Arkansas, who shared her knowledge about this family as well. Of course, my interest stems from the two related billboard monuments in Yarmouth, but I thoroughly enjoyed the multiple exchanges with Craig, Abby, and Teresa. We now have a significant amount of material on the Hills and Sargents of Arkansas and Maine. Still, a few curiosities remain.

1. James's wife, Mary, died in 1853, six years before James had the bill-board made. Why didn't he list her on the billboard as well? Was it simply that he wanted the billboard only for his siblings and parents? She died 11 years before him and her name is in a secondary position as "his wife" on their shared marker. The marker is nicely done, with curved and arched lines. The tympanum features a leafy design in bas relief, but a closer look shows a mix of two different plants. On the left side there are oak leaves with acorns, suggesting James's maturity at reaching age 72; one acorn is falling, symbolizing the end of his life. On the right side is a berried vine, suggesting Mary's maturity. The leaves are framed top and bottom with the words "Joined above" and "Parted below." All of this suggests to me that the marker was placed after James's death, not Mary's, and it leaves me wondering if James had originally marked Mary's grave with a distinct monument of her own.

Grave marker for James and Mary Hill at Hillside Cemetery.

2. James's mother, Sarah, died in 1845 and is listed on the billboard's third panel (the "Father & Mother" one), yet she has her own individual slate marker adjacent to the billboard. Why is she the only one to have two gravestones, why doesn't James's father have his own marker (he died 1850), and why wasn't the slate pulled once the billboard was erected?

3. James had seven of his siblings memorialized on the first two panels of the billboard, and their names are listed in the chronological order of their deaths, but one sibling is missing—his sister Mary who died in 1856. She died just three years before the monument was made and there was certainly room for her name at the end of

the second panel. But that last space was instead inscribed with the name Samuel Stockin, who was James's brother-in-law (that is, his wife's younger brother). Was it because Mary had married and was not buried in Yarmouth? Craig Stinson thinks that James probably just left her memorialization to her husband, Levi Webster. She'd married him in 1837 and had five children. The 1850 census has the five of them in Yarmouth in 1850, but after that I lost track of her.

Recall from Chapter 5 that two of James and Mary's sons were business partners of Cyrus Sargent, and that their daughter Mary was Sargent's first wife. As noted above, the Hill billboard is located just inside the gate off Hillside Avenue; the Sargent billboard is found in the center of the cemetery by walking straight up the central lane from the gate. Three markers for the Hills are located in a line immediately next to the Sargent monument. Closest to the billboard is a shared marker for James's son Augustus (died 1821, age 4) and daughter Olive (died 1831, age 1). James and Mary's marker with the leafy design is closest to the lane. Sandwiched in between is a marble obelisk for their firstborn son, Alexander Greenwood Hill.

ALEXANDER GREENWOOD HILL (1812–1847)

The story behind Alexander's accidental death is quite sad, and worth telling here. It was the summer of 1847, and he was living in Champagnolle, Arkansas—the same town where his sister Mary was living with her husband, Cyrus Sargent, and their first child, two-year-old Alice. Mary was pregnant with her second child, Elinor.

Alexander was heading back to Maine, traveling down the Ouachita River aboard the Steamer *Edna*. There were more than 50 passengers and crew making the journey. About halfway to New Orleans, all four of its boilers exploded, killing two dozen and wounding a half dozen more. Twenty-six were saved, including Dr. John B. Lewis of South Carolina, who wrote a letter to the *Weekly Raleigh Register* in order to give a first-hand account of the disaster.

Lewis harshly criticized the ship's crew, writing the disaster had presented "another lamentable exhibition of that recklessness of conduct, which too frequently characterizes those individuals having charge of the lives and property of the traveling community." He said that the conduct of the crew—operating under a "state of excitement" and under the influence of "ardent spirits"—was the subject of conversation by everyone on board.

Lewis noted that there had been an unusual whizzing sound coming from the boat as it approached the wharf at Columbia, Louisiana. While docked for 45 minutes, no water was thrown on the boilers to cool them. As the *Edna* pulled away to continue the journey south, the boilers exploded, "shivering the boat into countless fragments, tearing the boilers into numerous pieces and throwing them from one to four hundred yards." Of the victims of the tragedy, he wrote, "The groans of the wounded and shrieks of the drowning exceeded description." Seventeen bodies had been recovered at the time of Lewis's account; Alexander Hill was among them, and his body was brought home to Yarmouth for burial. He left behind a wife and six-year-old son.

Monument Makers: Hunt & Jewett

The Hill billboard is special not only because it is dated, but because it contains a signature of its maker. When midcentury marble workers signed monuments, they typically placed their names in the lower right corner, above ground level, for all to see. Despite examining the Hill billboard firsthand at least a half dozen times, the worn surface and heavy lichen led me to miss the faded evidence of its maker's mark. But finally, after carefully studying the surface of the stone, I discovered a very faint two-line mark. After comparing it to other clearer signature marks on other stones from the period, I settled on "Hunt & Jewett" with "Portland" just underneath. This is one of the more commonly seen signatures on gravestones produced in southern Maine in the 1850s and 1860s. The Hunt was Richard K. Hunt, the Jewett was James M. Jewett, and they had a marble monument shop on Congress Street in Portland.

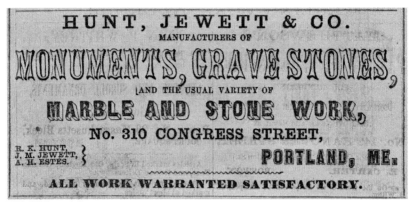

Typical ad for the Portland marble shop of Hunt & Jewett from 1855.

These two men were of different generations; Richard Hunt became James Jewett's father-in-law when James married Asenath Hunt in 1847. In the spring of 1849, the first advertisement for their new company appeared as "Hunt, Jewett, and Estes." Albert Estes was James's age and he must have been holding down the fort at the beginning of their partnership, since the 1850 census for Bridgton (40 miles from Portland) had Richard Hunt and James Jewett living in the same household there. That census was recorded on August 12. The census in Portland was recorded eight days later, and James Jewett was listed as a stonecutter boarding with a half dozen other young people. Estes left the business in the mid-1850s.

AWARD-WINNING MARBLE WORK

In 1851, James Jewett joined the Maine Charitable Mechanic Association. Their membership roster listed him as a marble worker. The MCMA had been established in 1815 to assist local tradesman, and by the midcentury was flourishing. The organization held expositions to showcase the work and products of Maine's "mechanics," from shoemakers to boatbuilders to, of course, marble workers. At the 1854 exposition, the Hunt & Jewett company was awarded a bronze medal for its submission of a white marble gravestone. At the expo-

Front of the medal awarded to Hunt &
Jewett in 1859.

Reverse side of the medal awarded to
Hunt & Jewett in 1859.

sition in 1859, the same year they created the Hill family billboard, Richard Hunt and James Jewett were again awarded a bronze medal for their marble work. The medal can be seen today in the MCMA's wonderful library at Mechanics Hall on Congress Street, Portland.

Hunt & Jewett continued to supply area cemeteries with beautifully crafted marble grave markers into the early 1870s. A Portland newspaper article published October 22, 1864, promoted local marble workers and the manufacture of gravestones. Of Hunt & Jewett's Portland shop, the article noted, "Besides a large home demand, they have agents in every part of the state, and one or two traveling agents from whom orders are continuously being received...." That line is helpful since it confirms that monuments weren't just being made in local communities, but were being shipped statewide from at least one Portland shop.

A year after the promotional piece in the newspaper, James Jewett was cited for unpaid business taxes; he owed the city nearly $3,000. By 1868, he and Richard Hunt brought two other men into the business, but within a couple of months one withdrew due to ill health.

Hunt and Jewett worked and lived together for many years. Their families shared a home on Parris Street in Portland, which was first owned by the elder partner Hunt, but then changed hands in 1858 when Jewett purchased it from him. Mrs. Hunt died of consumption in 1870. The men worked with marble for just two more years, and then in 1872 ended their marble business. They stayed together, though, working as commission merchants buying and selling manufactured goods such as tobacco, sugar, and gunpowder. Still, it seems that things started to go downhill for the pair around this time.

TROUBLE ABOUT A HOUSE

A newspaper article from 1877 described the following scene at the Jewett house:

TROUBLE ABOUT A HOUSE.—Yesterday after-noon Constable Hall took possession of house No. 3 Parris street by virtue of the foreclosure of a mortgage. The house was occupied by James M. Jewett's family, and they refused to leave. Force won'du't work and persuasion was of no use. Several policemen were called but they refused to interfere. Deputy Marshal Black was sent for and told to clear the house, but he properly told them it was a civil case, and he should not meddle. Then several law-yers were sent for and a compromise was effect-ed.

Jewett foreclosure detailed in the Portland Daily Press, *June 5, 1877.*

The following year, Richard Hunt died of consumption at the age of 73. There's no sign of James Jewett in Portland after that. In the 1880 census for Portland he was not found, yet his wife, Asenath, was listed as head of household, and one of their daughters was living with her. Perhaps they separated or divorced, but in any case it appears he died in Ellsworth, Maine, in 1890. Asenath Jewett died in San Francisco in 1901; she was living there with another of their daughters. Her cremains were interred at the historic San Francisco Columbarium.

The Hills and the Sargents: Final Words

The Hills and Sargents of Yarmouth, Maine, were intertwined by marriage, business, and, ultimately, their interesting gravestones at Hillside Cemetery. Teresa Harris's reflection about them brings their stories in my book to an end. She wrote, "These families were multifaceted, they were successful land speculators, active in religious circles, socially interesting, productive businessmen, politically active and several supported the South during the Civil War. We may never fully understand that dynamic, why some retained their ties to Maine and others remained residents of the South. The pull of home and its memories were still strong in the hearts of some, and perhaps they thought they might move back to Maine later. Their interesting personalities drew me deeply into their lives." It seems they drew me in as well.

CHAPTER 7

SLATE BILLBOARDS

*T*he dozen billboards detailed in previous chapters have had two main things in common: the slabs are marble and are held aloft by being fit into slotted granite posts. This chapter introduces a new material—slate—and a new construction method—billboards that are attached to their granite posts by metal hooks.

There are only three slate billboards in the Maine collection (see Chapter 8 for details about the third). Though undated and unsigned, I've assigned production dates of 1846 to 1849 for the three of them, based on their inscription and family details. It makes sense that the earlier billboards are made of slate; as noted in the Introduction, the entire gravestone-producing industry had evolved from slate to marble during the midcentury period of the 1840s to the 1860s.

THE BLANCHARD FAMILY MONUMENT, CUMBERLAND CENTER

The Blanchard family monument is one of three billboards located at the Congregational Cemetery in Cumberland Center. With respect to size, it is equal to Cyrus Sargent's marble billboard in Yarmouth as the longest stone at seven feet in length. It is nearly two feet tall and weighs about 325 pounds. Slate is a denser stone than marble and, when compared to a marble marker of equal size, weighs more. If the Blanchard stone was marble instead of slate, it would weigh about 300 pounds.

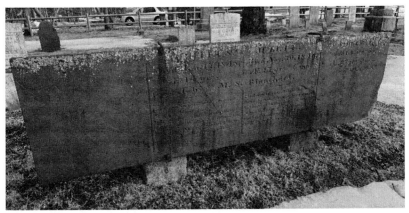

The slate billboard for the Blanchard family at Cumberland Center.

Also note the difference in the construction details from previous examples. In this case, the granite posts were placed much closer together than for slotted post billboards. Each post was fitted with two metal hooks that hold the slab in place. The slate appears sound, but rust stains are visible and both posts have cracks emanating from their top center surfaces where the metal hooks were embedded.

One of the most commonly seen problems with nineteenth-century marble tablet markers is the failure of the metal pins that were used to attach the stone to their bases. With continuous exposure to moisture, those metal pins corrode and ultimately burst. It's easy to find them—most have two visible breaks at

Back side of the Blanchard monument. Granite posts are closer together than for billboards with slotted posts. Note the top of the right post has broken away.

the bottom of the stone. In worst-case situations, the breaks are severe enough to cause the tablet to completely fall over. When repairing

A marble tablet marker undergoing conservation. Note the corroded pins have caused cracks in the stone. Photo courtesy of Janet Alexander.

those markers today, conservationists usually remove the corroded pins and either replace them with a non-corrosive pin or just make the necessary repairs to the stone itself without replacing them.

In the case of the Blanchard monument, the metal hooks at the tops of the posts are completely exposed to the elements. The flat tops of the posts allow water to pool and seep in around them. As a result,

Detail of the Blanchard billboard. Note cracks in the post emanating from where the metal hook was set.

60

both posts have cracks where the metal hooks have corroded and expanded; one post has completely broken where the hook burst, and a good chunk of the granite has fallen away.

ANDREW AND MYRA (SWEETSER) BLANCHARD

Andrew Gray Blanchard was born in 1797, Myra Sweetser in 1798. They married in 1824 and had at least eight children (two sons and six daughters) over an 18-year period. Andrew is among the many who petitioned for the town of Cumberland to be set off from North Yarmouth in 1820, also the year of Maine statehood. In the 1850 census for Cumberland, Andrew was listed as a farmer.

Their daughter Julia Frances died in 1846 at the age of 17; daughter Ardella Sweetser died in 1848 at age 14. The billboard was likely erected soon after Ardella's death. The slate has been divided into four panels. Inscriptions for Ardella and Julia are on the two center panels and a line reading, "Dau's of A. G. & M. S. Blanchard" runs underneath (and connects) the two. Each girl's panel also contains six lines of rhyming religious verse. The lettering and numbering of these inscriptions match and were clearly done at the same time by the same maker.

I date this billboard 1848 to 1849 because the third child memorialized, Andrew Gray Jr., died in 1855 at age 23 and was added to the monument by a different stonecutter. His inscription is found on the fourth panel, far right. The line below his name reads, "Son of A.G. & M.S.B.," but no verse similar to those inscribed for his sisters follows.

The first panel is blank and was probably originally intended for the parents themselves. If this monument had been erected only for the children in the family, Julia and Ardella would more likely have been listed on the first and second panels rather than second and third. In any event, the patriarch Andrew followed his namesake son's death by a year. Rather than being added to the billboard, he was buried nearby with his own marker as "Capt. Andrew G. Blanchard." Myra lived nearly three decades more, but when she died in 1884 she too was buried nearby with her own marker. That first panel, slightly larger than the other three, was just never used.

THE SCHELLINGER FAMILY MONUMENT, POLAND

The second slate billboard with granite posts and metal hooks is found at the Locust (or sometimes Locust Grove) Cemetery in Poland. A simple edge was carved along the border of the surface, serving as a decorative frame around the four panels of inscription. Each of the four panels memorializes one member of the Schellinger family: the patriarch's wife, son, daughter, and daughter-in-law. Their deaths occurred between 1835 and 1845, and I believe the billboard was made in the 1846 to 1849 period.

The Schellinger billboard at Locust Cemetery.

The monument's slab is six feet wide by two feet tall and weighs nearly 300 pounds. As is the case with the Blanchard billboard, the posts were placed more closely together in order to allow the stone to be attached by the hooks. However, unlike the Blanchard stone, the upper hooks emerge from the front of the posts instead of the top. They're located a few inches from the top; it's a simple difference that has allowed them to be less exposed to the elements, and therefore slowed down the process of corrosion. Thus far, these posts have avoided the cracking and breaking that the Blanchard posts have experienced.

The post and hook construction of the Schellinger billboard.

THE FAMILY

William Schellinger (born 1775) and Elizabeth (Betsey) Waterhouse (born 1783) were married in 1805. Records for only three children have been found: William Jr. (b. 1806), Polly (b. 1808), and John (b. 1815). The gap between Polly's and John's births leads me to wonder if there might have been two or three others. The three known children all reached adulthood. In fact, William Jr. lived to age 92. A few years before his death, he was interviewed for the book *Poland Centennial*, published in 1896 to celebrate the centennial of the town of Poland, Maine. He was described as being "still in rugged condition," and having a mind that was "very clear as regards the early history of Poland." He described how, as a little boy, he was sent out to the corn fields following late frosts to trim dead leaves from the stalks in order to help the corn restart growth. In better crop years, he recalled single evenings when 300 bushels of corn were husked and "a considerable amount of New England rum disposed of at the same time." As well, he recalled "the baking ovens of those days, which were made of stones piled on a large flat rock or ledge, on which a large quantity of dry wood was burned, and which sufficiently heated them to bake the pots of beans and loaves of bread."

When William Jr. died in 1898, he was buried at Locust Cemetery in a grave marked with his own stone. But his first wife, Mary, is on the billboard. Her name and details are on the third of the four panels. She predeceased him by over 60 years; his second wife, Desire, is also at Locust with her own marker.

The first panel holds the name of William Sr.'s wife, Elizabeth. She passed in 1837 at the age of 54. William Sr. died in 1852 and has his own marker at Locust Cemetery. William Jr.'s sister Polly has the second panel and brother John has the fourth panel. Polly was unmarried and age 27 when she died in 1835; I believe John was also unmarried when he died at the age of 30 in 1845.

CHAPTER 8

MISSING PIECES

MISSING POSTS...

*T*wo of the three slate billboards in Maine are found at Poland's Locust Cemetery and were probably made in the same stone shop around the same time. The Glysson family monument featured in this chapter is similar to the nearby Schellinger one in that a simple decorative border frames the four inscription panels. It's almost the same size with respect to inscribable surface area, but it weighs 50 pounds less given that the slab's thickness is just 1.5 inches (most are two inches). My guess is that it was originally held aloft using posts and hooks like the other two. But today there are no posts; perhaps the hooks corroded and failed, causing the slab to

The Glysson family monument at Locust Cemetery is being held up by a new pair of pressure-treated wooden supports.

fall. If that is true, the posts must have been taken away, as I couldn't find any nearby. The slab is now being held above ground level on a pair of pressure-treated wood easel-like supports. But for some lichen growth, the slab itself seems to be in good condition.

THE GLYSSON FAMILY

Only two of the four panels on this slate are inscribed. The family patriarch, Sylvanus Barnes Glysson, was born in 1793 and died in 1835. He has the first panel. Sylvanus married Ruth True in New Gloucester in 1814, but she was never added to the billboard. Although vital records are somewhat inconsistent and therefore not fully reliable, up to a dozen children are found for Sylvanus and Ruth, born 1815 through 1835. What's clear is that when Sylvanus died in 1835 at the age of 42, he left Ruth with six children, three of whom were under the age of 5. In the 1840 census, she was listed as head-of-household with five children living with her. She must have relied heavily on her two adult sons for support, since she had not remarried and was caring for three kids under age 10. In 1850, she was still a single parent of five (they were by then aged 15 to 30). I lost track of Ruth after that, so I don't know when or where she died. Perhaps she ultimately did remarry, maybe she moved away, or maybe she died in Poland, but records of her death were lost or never created.

The second panel on the billboard names three of the Glysson children: Decatur (age 23), Lucy (age 16), and Rosamond (age 11), who died between 1829 and 1838. Under their names we find the words, "Sons and daughters of Sylvanus B. and Ruth Glysson." The two panels on the right side of the monument were never inscribed.

I spoke with Adam Strout, public works director for the town of Poland, who told me that Locust Cemetery received some much-needed attention from the Public Works Department a couple of years ago. While working at the cemetery, he found the Glysson billboard leaning against some shrubbery and buried partway in the dirt. He knew they couldn't leave it that way, so he crafted the pair of pres-

The front of the slate billboard for the Glysson family at Locust Cemetery. Lettering was cut very close to the surface of the stone and is difficult to read.

sure-treated wooden supports using a town office signpost that was no longer needed. It's a great example of recycling, and I think it is especially appropriate that wood that once held up a signboard now holds up a billboard.

A MISSING SLAB…

I've been poking around Portland's 350-year-old Eastern Cemetery for years, researching its history and many of its grave markers for my first two books, bringing hundreds of visitors through as part of the walking tours program I lead for Spirits Alive (the Friends of Eastern Cemetery), and creating training material for other tour guides. Despite having walked the landscape countless times, until recently I paid little attention to a pair of granite posts in the "new" section of the cemetery. That section was added to the original burying ground in 1795—hardly new by today's standards—but given that the cemetery was established 127 years earlier, in 1668, "new" works just fine as a descriptor when we bring visitors through on tours.

The new section was set up in an orderly fashion, with straight lines of graves and many family lots consisting of four to eight plots set off by granite posts fitted with chains or metal poles. Sadly, the new section has also suffered a great deal of abuse and neglect over the years, but since it is the area most visible to the public from Portland's main street, Congress Street, it has received a great deal of attention from the volunteer Conservation Crew of Spirits Alive, led by Martha Zimicki, who serves with me on the organization's board.

As my brain began to develop the idea that billboard monuments are actually a distinct monument type, I realized that those two posts in the new section were unlike the other posts serving simply as fencing around family lots. Instead they were cut with slots and located six feet apart—perfect for holding a large marble slab above ground—a billboard! But, there is no stone…

All that's left of the Huse billboard at Portland's Eastern Cemetery are the posts.

The two posts are upright and sound with solid, larger square bases. They are also fitted with capstones resembling pyramid hip roofs. The slots extend up to the caps, so while the whole finished posts look like those of a pocket-slot billboard, my guess is that they are probably of the drop-slot variety. If I'm right, the cap-less posts would have been placed first, then the marble slab dropped down into the slots, then the caps added as a finishing touch.

IDENTIFYING THE MONUMENT'S OWNER

I used the original survey map and burial records to figure out who owned the monument on this family lot. The cemetery was established in 1668, but no formal survey was conducted for over 200 years. Finally, in 1890, Portland's city engineer, William Goodwin, accomplished that task. He assigned section letters to the landscape and recorded all known graves. He created a cemetery plot map that we still use today during our conservation work. Whether purposely or accidentally, many stones have been moved around over the years; the Goodwin map helps us put markers back where they were originally placed (at least where they were found in 1890). Two sources of burial records exist: One is the William Jordan book with an alphabetical list, the other (more helpful for this task) is the *Record of Interments* (ROI), which provides a section-by-section, line-by-line, plot-by-plot list of burials known as of 1890.

The result of this sleuthing was that I identified the family as that of James Huse. He was born 1779 in Newburyport, Massachusetts. His wife, Lydia Lowell, was also born that year, but in New Casco, Maine.

THE HUSE FAMILY

James and Lydia married in Portland in 1802. Nine children were born between 1803 and 1821. James, a "housewright" (or house carpenter), was one of the founding members of the Maine Charitable Mechanic Association in 1815. By 1823 he had become its vice president. Over the next two decades, James served in a variety of roles, including city district warden, surveyor of boards, and surveyor of mahogany and hard woods.

"Drunken in the Street"

James Huse was a member of the Third Congregational Church in Portland, and in the winter of 1833–1834 became embroiled in a scandal regarding the church and the Portland newspaper *Christian Pilot*. It seems the *Pilot* had made a contract with a man named Daniel C. Colesworthy to print the weekly paper. He was also a member of the Third Congregational Church. Apparently some leaders of the church disagreed with the manner in which the paper reflected the church's doctrine; specifically, those concerns were documented by the church scribe as "some of the articles of faith adopted by this church are habitually misrepresented and denied, and errors in doctrine...are professedly defended."

So, on January 27, 1834, the church called Mr. Colesworthy to appear before its leaders (James Huse among them) to answer a charge that he had "breached his express covenant agreement." Mr. Colesworthy defended himself by stating that he simply had a contract to print the newspaper, he had no interest in the content, and he felt obligated to fulfill his contract. The church leaders gave him an ultimatum: stop printing the paper or be excommunicated from the church. He told them he just wanted to do his job and the church leaders voted to excommunicate him from the church.

The editors of the *Christian Pilot* were outraged and in the subsequent weeks filled columns with what they called "public debate" over the issue. In the February 13 issue, they pointed out the absurdity of the decision of the church, arguing for Mr. Colesworthy, "Had he merely been detected in an act of injustice, or a series of fraudulent conduct, or habitual falsehood—or had he been seen *drunken in the street*...." But no, his excommunication was for the "*aggravated crime* of printing a religious newspaper!" It was the line "drunken in the street" that brings James Huse into this issue. Further into that particular article, the paper expressed its duty to the public to print the names of those in the Third Church who had either voted for or supported Colesworthy's excommunication. And on that list of 18, with the only name printed in capital letters, was "JAMES HUSE." Just after his name, there was a parenthetical quote attributed to him: "I should rather see him drunk in the street, than he should print the *Christian Pilot.*"

The following column entitled "MR. JAMES HUSE" appeared in the March 6, 1834, edition of the paper:

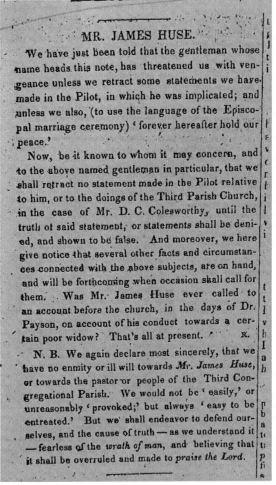

MR. JAMES HUSE.

We have just been told that the gentleman whose name heads this note, has threatened us with vengeance unless we retract some statements we have made in the Pilot, in which he was implicated; and unless we also, (to use the language of the Episcopal marriage ceremony) 'forever hereafter hold our peace.'

Now, be it known to whom it may concern, and to the above named gentleman in particular, that we shall retract no statement made in the Pilot relative to him, or to the doings of the Third Parish Church, in the case of Mr. D. C. Colesworthy, until the truth of said statement, or statements shall be denied, and shown to be false. And moreover, we here give notice that several other facts and circumstances connected with the above subjects, are on hand, and will be forthcoming when occasion shall call for them. Was Mr. James Huse ever called to an account before the church, in the days of Dr. Payson, on account of his conduct towards a certain poor widow? That's all at present. R.

N. B. We again declare most sincerely, that we have no enmity or ill will towards *Mr. James Huse,* or towards the pastor or people of the Third Congregational Parish. We would not be 'easily,' or unreasonably 'provoked;' but always 'easy to be entreated.' But we shall endeavor to defend ourselves, and the cause of truth — as we understand it — fearless of the *wrath of man,* and believing that it shall be overruled and made to *praise the Lord.*

Editor's column published March 6, 1834, that addressed the dispute the paper had with James Huse.

It seems that the editors had a bone to pick with James Huse—his name was the only one specifically highlighted in the earlier edition and they'd asked the somewhat snide question regarding the "poor widow" in this one. While it provides an interesting diversion from our study of the Huse billboard at Eastern Cemetery, we return to the subject at hand.

The Members of the Family on the Billboard

According to the ROI, these were the seven names listed on the Huse family billboard. Birth and death dates were apparently also inscribed on the stone, but I summarize here with just death year and age:

- James (patriarch), 1864, age 84
- Lydia Lowell (matriarch), 1858, age 78
  and their children:
- Emeline, 1843, age 38
- Lydia L., 1834, age 28
- James, 1827, age 18
- George L., 1831, age 18
- Joseph L., 1842, age 27

Emeline's name appeared on the billboard as Emeline Huse, but she was actually buried in Newburyport, Massachusetts, with a grave marker using her married name of Kimball. She had married Edward Kimball in 1828; he lived another 40 years after she passed and was buried beside her at the Oak Hill Cemetery in Newburyport.

Lydia L. was also married, but according to the ROI she was listed as Huse. She married Royal P. Locke in Buxton less than two years before she died. He appears to have left Maine and moved west after she passed away.

Of the three boys, a vital record of marriage was found only for Joseph; he wed Martha Duran in 1840. Joseph's vital record of death provides his cause of death as consumption.

William Huse (1810–1881)

In 1810, Lydia Huse had given birth to her fifth child, a son named William. He is the most likely member of the family to have erected the monument at Eastern Cemetery for his parents and siblings. He lived a full life of over 70 years in Portland, he had been close to his father (owning a company, James Huse & Son, with him for a few years), he had buried his first wife and some children at Eastern Cemetery,[12] and his three surviving siblings were not in the area at the time of their father's death in 1864.

In chatting with Martha Zimicki, I asked about the possibility that some pieces of the Huse billboard may have been buried in the area surrounding the two posts. Probing the ground near them has been added to the list of projects for the 2020 conservation season, just in case there are some fragments to be recovered.

Missing Post Caps (and a Photo)…

The Tapley family monument at Bass Cove Cemetery in Kennebunkport is a six-foot-wide marble drop-slot billboard weighing about 275 pounds. It has a full break through the center of the slab that has been repaired. When I first visited this billboard I noticed holes drilled in the top center

Note the drilled tops of the Tapley monument posts, which likely supported decorative caps.

of each post. My initial thought was that they might have once been decorated with urns. But the Huse monument in Portland—with

---

12. William ended up at Evergreen Cemetery across town when he died in 1881 at age 71.

its pyramidal capstones—led me to change my mind. I've decided that the missing pieces were not urns, but capstones.

The Tapley monument has suffered another loss, however. The panel that holds the name of the patriarch's namesake son, Tristram, has a photo pocket that is now empty. Photography began in the same period that the billboard monuments were being produced. Daguerreotype and tin type photos were made on metal plates, not paper, and so a new trend arose: adding photographs of the deceased (sometimes postmortem ones) to gravestones. Despite being made of sturdy metal, few of these photographs have survived the weather (or vandals). Still, the evidence of the popularity of this trend can be found on many midcentury gravestones. In fact, two billboard monuments in the Maine collection were produced with photo pockets, though both are now empty.

The Tapley monument's panel for son Tristram, which originally held his photograph.

The Tapley Family

Tristram Tapley and Lavinia Harris married in 1832. They had six children between 1833 and 1848. According to the 1850 and 1860 census records, Tristram was a caulker—probably working in Kennebunk's robust shipbuilding industry.

Though no date or maker's mark is found on the stone, I've assigned a production date of 1862. The slab has three panels. The center and right-hand panels appear to have been inscribed by the same hand and memorialize five of the six Tapley children who died between 1849 and 1861. The center panel has three who died young in the 1840s. The right-hand panel names son Tristram, who died in 1860 at age 24 (his name appears just below the empty photo pocket), and his sister Frances, who died in 1861 at age 17. There's a carver error on that panel too: Tristram's name is missing the second "r." His vital record gave the cause of death as dropsy (today, edema).

The Tapley family billboard at Kennebunkport.

The first panel of the billboard was likely left uninscribed for 30 years, reserved for Tristram and Lavinia. Their daughter Lucinda outlived all of her siblings and is their only child to live beyond her twenties. She became a schoolteacher and never married. She died at age 38 in 1874. Her name appears at the bottom of that first panel, below her father's and mother's names. Tristram died in 1886 (age 77) and Lavinia died in 1895 (age 88), but Lavinia's name was inscribed as "Lavinia B. Libby." I knew her family name was Harris, not Libby, so down the next rabbit hole I went to discover what this was about.

CHASING LAVINIA

I retraced the paper trail for the Tapleys and found that the 1850 census was clear: the Kennebunkport household consisted of Tristram Tapley, Lavinia Tapley, and three children. The 1860 census followed suit, Tristram, Lavinia, and two kids, all under the surname Tapley. But something had happened to the family in the 1860s, because the 1870 census had Tristram living 50 miles north in Brownfield, Maine, on the farm owned by Lavinia's brother Sylvester Harris. Lavinia was not there. I finally found her via her only surviving daughter, Lucinda. The 1870 census for Gorham, Maine, had a household of three people, Lewis Libby, "Lauria" Libby, and Lucinda Tapley. It appeared that a poor transcription had Lavinia listed as Lauria.

From there, I searched for marriage and divorce records, and finally got a match. In 1868, Lavinia sought a divorce from Tristram. My curiosity led me to the Maine State Archives in Augusta in order to learn details, and I was able to get a copy of the file, which read in part:

> ...she was married to the said Tristram on the 28th day of November AD 1832, that she has had six children by said Tristram, five of whom are now dead and the other is of age; that since their intermarriage has always behaved herself as a faithful and affectionate wife; but that Tristram, wholly regardless of his marriage covenant, during the past three years has

not contributed to the support of his family, but on the contrary has obliged the said Lavinia to support him in idleness. Also that the said Tristram has assaulted and otherwise cruelly treated her—and that his conduct in general, is such as prevents [her] from earning her livelihood. [Lavinia] prays that the bonds of matrimony may be dissolved between herself and the said Tristram.

She was granted her request. Divorce was not common in the nineteenth century. According to a report issued by the US Department of Health, Education, and Welfare in 1973, divorces in Maine in 1870 (just two years after the Tapley divorce and the first year such records were reported) occurred at the rate of six for every 10,000 people. Today's rate is much greater.

Between 1870 and 1880, Lavinia's new husband, Lewis Libby, must have died, for she appeared in the 1880 census living with her brother Sylvester Harris in Brownfield. Tristram was living in Winterport, Maine, with his new wife and her son from a previous marriage. Lavinia B. Harris Tapley Libby died in 1895. Her name appears under Tristram's on the billboard with the inscription "his wife" but uses her second husband's surname of Libby.

Chapter 9

THE ONES WITH THE METAL POLES

*T*hree marble billboards located within a short distance of each other differ from the posted varieties examined in earlier chapters in that they are held above ground clamped by metal poles. These were undoubtedly made by the same man, given how unique the poles/clamps are from other billboards and that the three are found in cemeteries within a geographic circle about six miles across in the towns of Bridgton and Harrison.

The Jackson Family Monument, Harrison

The first of this interesting trio is for Richard Jackson, his first wife, Mary, and their daughter Rebecah. It's a three-panel slab nearly six feet wide with a dry weight of about 325 pounds. Its great weight puts a lot of downward pressure on the metal clamps, and indeed there is a stress crack in the marble near one of the clamps.

This monument is at the South Harrison Cemetery in the town of Harrison. It was probably carved in the early 1860s, soon after Richard died, and intended only for these three members of the family. If you look closely at the panels, you'll see that they are not of equal size.

It seems that the carver fit the panels around the names, as opposed to creating three same-sized inscription panels and then fitting names into each space. Richard's is the largest panel since the name banner gives his first and family names.

The Jackson family billboard in Harrison.

The records for this family are sparse, but a vital record of their 1822 marriage exists for Richard Jackson and Mary K. Ingalls, both of Harrison. Children born to them is an issue less clear, although the billboard includes "their daughter" Rebecah K., who died in December of 1847 at age 19. That puts her year of birth at 1828. The 1830 census for Bridgton has a Richard Jackson family of five that includes a daughter in the age range of "under 5" and an adult female in the age range of "20 through 29"—good matches for Rebecah and Mary. But there's a mismatch for Richard. The census has one adult male in the age range of "20 through 29." If we are to believe the date on the billboard, he would have been 33 at the time the 1830 census was recorded. In any event, the billboard provides Mary's details of death: she passed at the age of 38 in 1841.

There's a possibility that Richard remarried a woman named Irene and had more children with her. The other possibility is that there was more than one Richard Jackson of the same generation living in that area in the midcentury. I tend to think the latter is the more likely situation. There is a vital record for an Irene Jackson, wife of a Richard Jackson who died in 1850. Since her year of death falls within the range of dates for the three listed on this billboard, I would think her name would have been included on the stone if she was part of this particular family.

The Hazen Family Monument, Bridgton

The second example of the pole and clamp billboards is very similar to the first, only larger. The Hazen family monument is a four-panel marble slab found at the Sweden Road Cemetery in Bridgton. The marble itself is almost seven feet wide and has a weight of about 350 pounds. There is at least one stress fracture near one of the clamps.

The Hazen family billboard in Bridgton.

This monument was erected for three children of Enoch and Martha Hazen, plus Martha Hazen's sister. Their dates of death span just five years, from 1826 to 1831, but I believe the monument was made in the early 1860s when the other two pole and clamp stones were produced. So, I consider this to be a backdated marker.

The family patriarch, Enoch Hazen, was born in Massachusetts in 1770; his wife, Martha A. Thompson, was born in Massachusetts in 1774. They married in Roxbury in 1797 and soon thereafter relocated to Maine (the vital record for their first child indicates his birth in Maine in 1799). Seven children are known to have been born to them, between 1799 and 1813.

Detail of the metal clamp and pole from the Hazen monument.

The first three panels name three of the children. First is son William, who died unmarried at the age of 24 in 1826. Second is daughter Theoda, who died unmarried in 1828 at the age of 24. Son Thomas also died in 1828, just six months after his sister, but his name does not appear on the billboard. The fact that he was not listed supports that this is a backdated monument. My guess is that Thomas has his own marker somewhere (if only I could find it!) and so there was no need to list him with the others. Thomas died at 28 and left behind a young wife and at least one child. The third panel is for daughter Mary, who died in 1828 at the age of 22. Mary's inscription reads, "Wife of William Potter." She had been married just six months when she died.

The final panel is for Jane (Thompson) Barnes, older sister of Martha (Thompson) Hazen. Her inscription reads, "Wife of Col. William Barnes of Roxbury, Mass." Perhaps Jane was visiting her sister in Bridgton when she passed and was buried there. Her death occurred a full generation before embalming was perfected. Until preservation of remains became common practice, bodies needed to be buried quickly for obvious reasons, and so people were just buried where they died. We find many markers from this period with inscriptions that include the deceased's home town.

PROHIBITION IN BRIDGTON

Though the full-blown national debate regarding prohibition of alcohol didn't begin until a bit later, Maine passed a law in 1846 that prohibited the sale of alcohol (except for medicinal purposes). In 1847, Enoch Hazen of Bridgton helped set the local debate into motion. His name appeared in a Portland newspaper as the lead petitioner (along with 45 unnamed others from the town of Bridgton) requesting that the state repeal the law "restricting sale of intoxicating drinks." Of course, within three years, Neal Dow would become mayor of Portland and the "Father of Prohibition," setting the national stage for what would become a decades-long struggle over the issue of temperance.

Enoch Hazen died in 1853; Martha followed in 1860. Their graves are found at Sweden Road Cemetery, just in front of the billboard and marked by a pair of beautifully decorated gravestones. I suspect their son John Hazen was responsible for erecting the billboard monument and the stones for his parents. John was in his 40s when his parents died; he lived to 1878 and is buried at Sweden Road along with his wife and at least two of their children.

The front of the 1861 Thompson billboard in Bridgton.

THE THOMPSON MONUMENT, BRIDGTON

The final pole and clamp billboard memorializes a couple, Archibald and Abigail Thompson. It's found at the front of the High Street Cemetery in Bridgton and has an interesting double-peaked top to the slab. It's on the small size for a billboard, at three feet wide by two feet tall, and weighs about 165 pounds. The poles and clamps are of the same design and material as the two larger monuments just described. But this marker is quite charming for the fact that it is recycled!

Archibald Thompson was born in 1782 in Bridgewater, Massachusetts.[13] He married Abigail Emerson sometime in the first

---

13. Despite the proximity of his monument to that of Martha Thompson Hazen just addressed, and that they are of the same generation and both born in Massachusetts, I was unable to find a familial link between them.

decade of the 1800s, and at least nine children were born into the family through 1831. Archibald briefly represented Bridgton in the Maine House of Representatives in the 1830s. In 1837, his daughter Mary married and his son John died under unusual circumstances. An Augusta newspaper reported his death on May 13: "Near the sources of the St. Croix, in the woods, John Thompson, son of Archibald Thompson, Esq. of Bridgton, age 25. Mr. Thompson had been in the wilderness getting out timber on a contract, when on the 18th of April, he was suddenly attacked by a fit, and died almost instantly. He was an enterprising, steady and highly respectable young man, and his decease has brought deep affliction to the hearts of his bereaved parents, brothers, sisters and other relatives and friends."

THE ANTI-SLAVERY SOCIETY OF BRIDGTON

Prohibition wasn't the only important national issue with a link to the families memorialized on Bridgton's billboard monuments. In 1846, Archibald Thompson played a key role during a meeting of the Anti-Slavery Society of Bridgton, though not on the side of the abolitionists. Instead, he was among the mob that tried to prevent the Society from meeting. An eyewitness to the event sent the *Portland Daily Advertiser* a letter describing what occurred at the meeting on June 3. The two-column article was titled "MOB IN BRIDGTON."

The meeting was held in the former Congregational Meeting House, which was then open for town meetings, public addresses, and other gatherings. A large crowd had gathered and Reverend J. P. Fessenden opened the meeting with a prayer and song. The president of the Society then addressed the attendees, reminding them to remain calm and orderly. The first-hand account reads:

> He had not concluded, when Nathaniel S. Littlefield, Esq.... entered the house, followed by Archibald Thompson, Esq. Ex-Representative of the town of Bridgton...and about twenty-five other individuals, whom their distinguished leader cer-

tainly cannot wish me to describe; not a few richly perfumed with the agreeable odor of New England.

Marching his redoubtable company up the broad aisle, Esq. Littlefield proclaimed that no discussion would be permitted in this place—that the people (looking round with complacency on the respectable company he had the honor to command) had so determined, and so it should be—that we had no right to hold such meetings, and that they should not be held in any public building in the town of B., if in any private house.

Being requested to point out what law we were violating by holding peaceable meetings, and exercising our right of free discussion—he stated, that there were many things which the law could not touch, that were still too bad to be tolerated, and must be put down. And when told by the President that he himself was violating the constitution and laws of the State of Maine by coming here to disturb a peaceful meeting, he replied, that he cared nothing about the constitution and the laws of the State of Maine—and that he came not here to argue, or to listen to argument, but to prevent it.

The Society president tried to bring order back to the meeting and invited Rev. Fessenden to make his remarks. The mob, including Archibald Thompson, raised such a noise that it was impossible for him to speak. The deputy sheriff accompanying Littlefield ordered the attendees to disperse. The abolitionists found it impossible to continue, and "thinking it better to suffer wrong for the time being than take the means of redress into their own hands, they adjourned to a private house where they held their meeting unmolested."

Archibald's Tablet Gravestone

Looking at the reverse side of the billboard shared by the Thompsons reveals that it has been recycled. It is fully inscribed to honor Archibald Thompson, who died at age 77 in 1859. There is a lengthy epitaph

The reverse side of the Thompson billboard, showing its original inscription from 1859, now sideways.

included. But the lines of inscription are at a 90-degree angle from the front of the monument. When Archibald died in 1859, his widow, Abigail (or another member of the family), had a large white marble gravestone made to mark his grave. It was tall and thin like the thousands of other standard marble markers made in the midcentury. The original plan at the time was probably to have a similar second marker made for Abigail whenever she might pass. But her death came relatively soon after her husband's; she died less than two years later, in 1861. I imagine two possibilities regarding the marker. First is that the family had Archibald's marker pulled up, the stonecutter then flipped it over, turned it 90 degrees to make it wider instead of taller, and cut the triangular tops into the stone. The second is that Archibald's marker was in the process of being made when Abigail died, leading the stonecutter to change the stone from a single monument to a double one. In either case, some of the lettering from the (original) reverse side was cut away.

Image turned 90 degrees to show original inscription for Archibald Thompson.

The three billboards using metal poles and clamps are certainly special for their unique method of holding the stones aloft, but this one is extra-special for being made of a recycled gravestone. I've scoured the cemeteries in the towns of Bridgton and Harrison in the hopes of finding more of these; perhaps someday someone else will find one tucked away from view.

CHAPTER 10

THE FOUR WIVES OF REUBEN SAWYER

One of the Cumberland Center billboards that set my obsession into motion is a large white marble slab hooked onto granite posts. It's divided into six panels and memorializes eight members of the Reuben Sawyer family, half of whom were his wives.

There were a few men named Reuben Sawyer in the area at the time our man was building his family. Other than the details provided on his marker, there's not a lot to be found about Reuben Sawyer of North Yarmouth (later Cumberland). He was born in 1784 or 1785 to Enoch and Mary (Sanborn) Sawyer. He served as executor of his father's last will and testament when he died in North Yarmouth in 1816, and then executor of the estate of his brother Nathaniel when he died there in 1820. As to occupation, I found no records. But with respect to his billboard monument, what sets Reuben Sawyer apart from everyone else in this book is that he was married four times and outlived all of his wives. Details of those marriages follow:

- First was in 1808 to Elizabeth Wyman (born 1786). He was 24, she was 22. One newspaper referred to her as "Miss" and another as "Mrs." They had two children; she died in 1816 at age 30.

- Second was in 1816 to Olive Shaw (born 1792). He was 32, she was 24. They had four or five children together. Theirs was the longest lasting marriage, at 15 years. She died in 1831 at age 39.
- Third was in 1832 to Susan Hill (born 1794). He was 48, she was 38. One daughter, named Olive for his second wife, was born to them. They may also have had a son. Theirs was the shortest marriage, at five years. Susan died in 1837 at age 43.
- The final marriage was in 1838 to Jane C. W. (no vital record was found to confirm her last name). He was 54, she was 43. No children were born. She died in 1846 at age 51.

The "Four Wives" billboard in Cumberland Center.

Reuben died in 1848 at the age of 64. His details are inscribed on the first panel of the billboard. The next four panels are for each of his four wives in the chronological order of their marriages. The final panel lists two children who died within two days of each other in April of 1843: Huldah, a 16-year-old daughter of Olive, and Olive, an eight-year-old daughter of Susan.

Structurally, the monument appears to be in good condition, though there is some staining and bleaching of the marble from the metal hooks that hold it to the granite posts.

MONUMENT MAKER: JOSEPH R. THOMPSON

About five miles from the Congregational Cemetery, close to the town line separating Cumberland and Falmouth, is the Foreside Community Churchyard Cemetery. Also called the "New Casco Cemetery," it's behind the church and easy to miss if you're driving too fast along that stretch of Route 88. It's at this cemetery that we find a marker signed by marble worker Joseph R. Thompson.

Thompson was one of the two successors to Bartlett Adams; he and partner Francis Ilsley took over the shop and stock of the Portland business when Adams died in 1828. Thompson was a lifelong gravestone maker. After Ilsley left the partnership in the early 1830s, Thompson operated his own business in Portland for decades, receiving multiple awards from the Maine Charitable Mechanic Association for his work. He became the organization's president in 1845. Thompson was sole proprietor of his business, which he frequently advertised in Portland newspapers and directories. Married and a family man, his son, Enoch, followed in his footsteps—he had his own stone shop on Cumberland Avenue and was in business through the turn of the twentieth century.

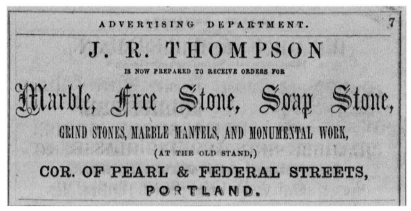

A typical advertisement from Joseph R. Thompson, 1855.

Thompson was in his prime during the time that the billboard monuments were being made. Though I haven't found his signature on any of them, I know he was the maker of the Reuben Sawyer monument and I suspect he made at least a half dozen others.

One day while wandering the Foreside churchyard, I discovered Thompson's signature on an 1848 marker for Amelia Ann Sturdivant. I took close-up photos of the marker in order to study Thompson's lettering and numbering.[14] Then, looking closely at the Sawyer billboard, I noticed similarities to the Sturdivant stone, and so I put close-up photos of each side by side to do the comparison.

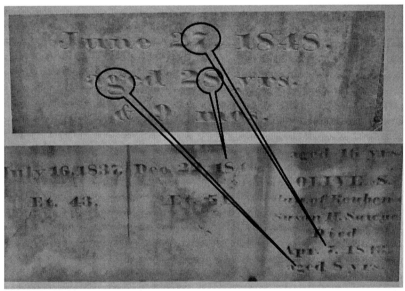

A comparison of Joseph Thompson's letters and numbers. Top stone is the Sturdivant marker which bears his signature. Bottom stone is the Sawyer billboard, which is unsigned.

We students of gravestones know that apprentice stonecutters learned the craft by copying the decorative carvings, lettering, and numbering of their masters. So there is a bit of a leap of faith when we identify a stone as carved by one worker over another based solely on letters. I've had good practice in this regard. For my first book (about

---

14. In my book *Early Gravestones in Southern Maine*, I wrote a chapter about Joseph Thompson that included photos of the Sturdivant signed stone. Please see that book for more images.

stonecutter Bartlett Adams), I studied thousands of gravestones to learn specific designs and letters in order to sort stones by the carvers working in his shop. Thompson surely had apprentices and others working in his shop too. But my confidence is high regarding Thompson being the maker of the Sawyer billboard—there are multiple matches in letters and numbers, the timing is right (that is, the Sturdivant and Sawyer stones were likely carved the same year), and the Thompson stone shop was the closest one to Cumberland Center when the billboard monument was made. With this attribution, I had confirmed two makers of these unique gravestones: the company Hunt & Jewett, and Joseph R. Thompson.

CHAPTER 11

THE EXTREMES

Maine's billboards exhibit a nice variety of differences in construction, design, and size. This chapter takes a look at three billboard extremes: the longest, the tallest, and the smallest.

THE LONGEST

The town of Wilton has the longest billboard monument—it's for the family of Levi Hardy. The cemetery's signboard reads "Weld Street Cemetery," MOCA lists it as the "Weld Road Cemetery" (which matches the actual street name, Weld Road) and the Find-a-Grave website calls it the "Wilton Old Town Cemetery." I asked the town's Historical Society for clarification, and that organization's Flossie Dere added one more to the list: "Old Village Cemetery." Flossie agreed that the use of various names by different parties creates some confusion. To help those who wish to see the Hardy monument confirm that they're at the right place, I use "Weld Street Cemetery," since it matches the sign on site.

The billboard is super long, consisting of two marble slabs fit into three pocket-slot type granite posts. Metal rods installed between the

The Hardy monument in Wilton, the longest of all known billboards in Maine.

posts have helped to keep the structure sound. Each slab is over six feet long but only 18 inches tall and weighs nearly 300 pounds. Adding the posts brings the monument's total width to 14 feet! The marble was cleaned during a MOCA-sponsored conservation workshop a few years ago and still looked great when I visited in the summer of 2019. There are three panels per slab, one of which has never been inscribed.

Levi Hardy (1809–1878)

The family patriarch was Levi Hardy, born on a Wilton farm in 1809. He married Eliza Drury of Temple, Maine, in 1831. Four children were born to them between 1833 and 1838. Eliza was 30 when she passed away in the spring of 1838. Her newborn son, Milton, died less than a month later. They may have been first buried with grave markers of their own, since I believe this monument was made after Levi died 40 years later.

Eliza's death left Levi caring for their three young kids, but he remarried within a year to Catherine Mosher. Catherine delivered four more children into this family, from 1840 to 1852. Her firstborn was named Vitellus Merrill Hardy, and he would live a long life of 85 years. Though he is not memorialized with the others on the billboard, his obituary from 1925 provides us with some information about life in the Hardy household during his youth.[15] It reads, in part:

> Dr. Hardy was born in Wilton, Me., Oct. 13, 1840, the son of Levi and Catherine Mosher Hardy. His early life was spent on the farm. He was educated in the rural schools taught by transient teachers, and by himself in his mother's kitchen. Thus he prepared himself for college. As he could not enter college because of financial reasons, he continued his college course by himself, with almost no aid from schools or teachers.

Levi died in 1878 at the age of 68. His second wife and five of his children survived him. Although I searched for probate records for the majority of the 38 families who have Maine billboard monuments, few exist. One exception was Levi Hardy, whose Franklin County probate file was found. I read through the file, hoping to identify a monument maker who had been paid for Levi's gravestone. The Hardy file is silent with regard to that, but did itemize some other final expenses. The estate paid $19 for a "coffin, box, & etc.," $5.50 to the cemetery sexton, and $2 for publishing the death notice in the newspaper. That no itemization was found for the monument itself suggests that either Levi Hardy had it placed years before he died or his surviving five children took care of that cost after he died. They certainly were a loving family; I was touched by this short handwritten note found in the file:

---

15. The original obituary was published in The Morrisville *Messenger*, a local paper in Vermont, where Vitellus (then a Reverend Doctor, having been awarded the degree of Doctor of Divinity from the University of Vermont) died at his advanced age. Some of the obituary was later published in a Hardy family genealogy from 1935 (see bibliography for details).

Wilton, 1878

To the Hon. Horace B. Prescott, Judge of Probate

The undersigned children and heirs of Levi Hardy, late of Wilton, deceased, respectfully request that all the personal estate of our late father be given as an allowance to our mother, Catherine Hardy.

Very respectfully,

The inscribed side of the Hardy billboard in Wilton.

SIX PANELS

There are three panels on each slab. Levi's name was inscribed on the center panel of the first slab. The next panel to the right holds the name of his first wife, Eliza (1808–1838), while the panel to the left is blank and was surely originally intended to hold the name of his second wife, Catherine. But after Levi's death, Catherine moved to Vermont to be with her daughter, and it was there that she died in 1897.

The second slab holds the names of the three children who predeceased him: Eliza's daughter Marion, who died in 1850 at age 17; Catherine's infant son Levi, who was born and died in 1844; and Eliza's infant son Milton, who was born and died in 1838.

THE TALLEST

Saco has the only billboard with a slab height that reaches a full three feet. It's for Polly and Dominicus Cutts, located in the beautiful Laurel Hill Cemetery, on a well-shaded slope toward the back of the property. If you visit in the spring, you'll be rewarded by the thousands upon thousands of daffodils blooming along the banks of the Saco River.

The marble slab is less than five feet wide, so it's the height of the stone that boosts its weight to 380 pounds. It is of the pocket-slot granite post variety and is in good condition, but could use a gentle cleaning.[16]

Dominicus Cutts was born in 1778; Mary (Polly) Chadbourne was born 1780. They married in 1832, but apparently had no children. Dominicus came from a well-to-do family in Saco (at the time called Pepperellborough). His father, Colonel Thomas Cutts, was a successful lumber mill owner and called "Saco's Most Eminent Citizen in the Country's Early Days" by biographer George Emery. The Saco River provided an ideal place for lumber mills, and Maine's claim to having the northernmost coastline in the colonies allowed trade ships to reach European ports more quickly than those embarking from the colonies to the south. The Saco Museum is worth visiting for many reasons; seeing the full-figure portraits of Colonel Cutts and his wife, Elizabeth Scamman Cutts, by John Brewster Jr. is certainly one of them.

Colonel Cutts owned a great deal of land in the area, including a large patch along the falls of the Saco River that was first known as

---

16. D-2 is the only nationally recognized biologic solution recommended for cleaning gravestones. For those unfamiliar with the proper materials and methods for cleaning stones, visit the MOCA or AGS websites.

The Cutts monument in Saco, the tallest of all known billboards in Maine.

Indian Island (since it was a place where the natives had historically gathered). It became known as Cutts Island under the colonel's ownership. Then, after he died in 1821, his son Dominicus sold the land to a Boston company, which put up a large cotton mill employing 500 workers. The island became known as Factory Island at that point, and is still referred to as such today. The Saco River flows on either side of the island, which is located between Biddeford and Saco. Today, the island contains restaurants, pubs, and historic buildings.

Dominicus was a sea captain; he and his brothers were all active in their father's mill and shipping enterprises. The family maintained good business records, and fortunately a large volume of papers exists, including personal correspondence between Dominicus and his brother Richard held in the collections of the Maine Maritime Museum in Bath.

Dominicus died at the age of 66 in 1844. Polly followed nine years later, passing at the age of 73. The billboard monument honors just the two of them, with Polly's name appearing first.

The Smallest

The last of our extremes is a cenotaph[17] at the Bass Cove Cemetery in Kennebunkport. It's for George H. Ward, who died in Charleston, South Carolina, in 1856 at the age of 36. Compared to all the others in the collection, it truly is small. It's less than three feet wide and just ten inches tall, so it has a dry weight of less than 60 pounds. It is of the drop-slot granite post variety, and it's unknown if a metal bar was installed on the posts, since the marker is being subsumed by the surrounding earth.

The Ward monument in Kennebunkport, the smallest of all known billboards in Maine.

The Ward family lot contains average-sized tablet markers for seven others in the family—George's parents, four siblings, and a brother-in-law. They are all in a line along the back edge of the family lot. His stone is in front of them, straddling the plots for his sister Adeline and

---

17. Cenotaph is a monument placed for a person whose remains are buried elsewhere.

brother Francis;[18] that placement further supports that George's body is not there.

George's birth year of 1820 is inferred from his grave marker, since no vital record was located. His father, Nathaniel Ward, was a boat builder; his mother, Sarah Miller, had married Nathaniel in 1815. George's father predeceased him by two years, but his mother outlived him by 25 years. No record of marriage was found for George, so existence of a spouse and/or children is in question.

The circumstances surrounding George's death in South Carolina have also eluded me. No vital record of death, newspaper notices, family genealogies, or other documents are found that might lend a clue. Searches on findagrave.com, ancestry.com, genealogybank.com, and familysearch.org left me scratching my head. I contacted the South Carolina Historical Society for help. They checked newspapers of the period, obituaries, and other files. They looked at deeds and directories to see if George had relocated there from Maine—again, nothing was found.

While I'd love to know more about what happened to George in Charleston, South Carolina, a paper trail has yet to emerge. And so, in the meantime, I remind myself that it is always good to have a few unexplained mysteries.

---

18. Francis's marker may actually be a cenotaph as well, for his inscription reads, "Died on his passage from Zanzibar, March 17, 1853, at the age of 27." It's likely that he was buried at sea.

CHAPTER 12

THE ONES WITH THE METAL FRAMES

THE PRINCE FAMILY MONUMENT, CUMBERLAND CENTER

*E*ach of the three billboards at the Congregational Cemetery in Cumberland adds a little spice to the mix. The Blanchard stone from Chapter 7 is unusual for its material—slate; the Sawyer stone from Chapter 10 for its family dynamic—four wives; and the Prince stone for its support structure—a metal frame.

The white marble slab for the Prince family is six feet wide and 325 pounds. It has six panels. I suspect the stonecutter was Joseph Thompson, based on a simple bouquet of flowers carved at top center of the stone that looks much like a few other designs from the same period that I know were his. These flowers are in a circled pane, which breaks up the usual, more linear, look of the majority of billboards. The key difference between this monument and all others is that it is held aloft by metal hooks on a metal frame. I *think* the metal frame is original to the monument, but I admit to having a lingering doubt about it. Overall, this billboard seems to be in good condition.

James Prince was born in 1776; his first wife, Sarah Drinkwater, in 1778. They married in 1801 and had 11 children over an 18-year

The Prince billboard at Cumberland Center.

Detail of the Prince monument, probably carved by Joseph Thompson.

period. Sarah died in 1824 at age 46, and is memorialized on the second panel as "wife of" James. Next to her is James's second wife, Eunice. She is listed as "widow of" James, but she wasn't a widow for very long, as James had died three weeks before her. He died in December of 1848 and she in January of 1849. Given the timing of their deaths, and the fact that the rest of the monument is fully inscribed with names of children who predeceased them, I'm confident in assigning a production date of 1849 to this billboard.

When James married Eunice Humphrey in 1825, he was a single father of 11 children. Eunice brought four more children into this large family. The Princes were apparently a hardy group; most of the

Reverse side of the Prince billboard, showing its metal frame.

15 children seem to have survived. Only three predeceased their father, and two of them had reached adulthood. Eunice's son Arthur died as a toddler in 1829 and is on the final panel. Occupying the fourth and fifth panels are children of Sarah: Leonora, who died in 1834 at age 19, and Cornelius, who died in 1842 at age 30.

THE RICH FAMILY MONUMENT, BUCKSPORT

Located more easterly than any other billboard in Maine, the Rich family monument is found at Riverview Cemetery in Bucksport. The marble slab is very similar to the billboards for the Mudgett and Houston children (see Chapter 4), in that the names of the children are carved in bas relief within banners at the top of each panel. Additionally, like those other two, there's a line that runs along the bottom of the stone that reads, "Children of..." (and in this case, "Jona. B. & E. W. Rich"). But where this marker departs from the others is in the structure created to hold the stone aloft. The Rich stone has an interesting pair of wrought iron supports, the upper loops of which extend above the stone and then circle back down to hold the stone in place.

Above: The Rich billboard in Bucksport.

Left: Detail of the Rich billboard showing looped metal support.

The marble is just over four feet wide and has a weight of about 150 pounds. There are some small stress fractures along the lower edge of the stone, and it has slipped a bit from the right side support. As a result, the right lower corner of the marker is resting on the ground and the whole thing is off-level.

Jonathan Baker Rich was born in Truro, Massachusetts, in 1806. Emeline W. Cobb was born c. 1811. They probably married in Massachusetts and then moved to Maine around 1831. The Portland paper ran a series of notices that year regarding letters being held at the Portland Post Office under Jonathan's name, so my guess is that they were still searching for a home. He became a mason. Records of births for the couple are sketchy, but I found at least eight children who I believe were theirs.

Reverse side of the Rich billboard, showing its unique metal support structure.

The four kids on the monument died between 1835 and 1850, all under age two. Emeline died of consumption in 1859 and was buried near her children at Riverview. Jonathan then remarried in 1860, to Sarah Howes. Jonathan died in 1876; he too was buried at Riverview. His gravestone is decorated with one of my favorite midcentury designs, a hand with a finger pointing toward heaven.

CHAPTER 13

TWO FENCED LOTS

*T*wo Maine billboards were built to serve a secondary purpose of fencing the burial lots of the families they memorialized. Setting private lots off from the rest of a cemetery is common. In early community graveyards that were truly open public spaces, families might stake out a patch they presumed would be sufficiently large enough for them. Towns that controlled access to their burying grounds might charge fees for measured lots containing multiple individual plots. And just as families could decorate a grave with the size, type, and style of gravestone they wanted, they could also fence their designated lots.

In colonial burying grounds, fencing would have been made of wood. Then, in the 1800s, stone posts were erected on the corners of some lots and finished with chains, poles, rods, or wooden rails; Eastern Cemetery in Portland has numerous surviving examples. Later in the century, when cast metal became popular, families marked the borders of their lots with metal fences decorated with repetitive patterns of lambs, praying children, flowers, or other designs and symbols of the day. Metal fences were also often fitted with gates that bore family names and dates, allowing visitors to step into the lot itself.

THE CHANDLER MONUMENT, JAY

Jacob and Love Chandler were buried in a two-person lot at Beans Corner Cemetery in Jay. Jacob died in 1842 at the advanced age of 79; Love died in 1853 at the even more advanced age of 83. The white marble slab inscribed with their names measures between four and five feet wide and weighs about 150 pounds. It was attached to granite posts with bolts. The stonecutter drilled through the slab and the granite posts in order to fit long metal rods from the front of the stone to the back of the rear posts on the lot. Note how all four posts are fit with metal rods running front to back and side to side to create a penned-in look. It's a small lot without a gate, so it was not designed for visitors. Like many other billboards, the slab on the Chandler monument has some stress fractures along its lower edge.

The fenced lot of Jacob and Love Chandler in Jay.

Jacob Chandler was born in 1763 in Westford, Massachusetts. Love Pease was also born that year—on Martha's Vineyard, into a large family of early settlers of the island. Love was actually Jacob's third wife. He'd been married to Rhoda Pollard for just three years when she died in 1787, soon after delivering her second child. Jacob married for the second time in 1792, to Judith Pettis, but she died about a year later without bringing any children into the family. No burial locations are known for either Rhoda or Judith. Jacob and Love were likely married in 1793, since records of the births of their five children begin in 1794. Their marriage persevered for 50 years.

Detail of the Chandler billboard.

Epitaphs are commonly found on tablet markers and were added to a few billboards as well. There's a Biblical verse carved on the Chandler monument that has a tender, sentimental meaning, but is somewhat off-putting as literally written. The verse is from Job 19:26. Inscribed on the stone is:

> Though after my skin worms destroy this body
> Yet in my flesh shall I see God.

The meaning of this verse (if I may be an amateur biblical scholar for just a moment) is that the soul outlasts the body, a theme that is present on gravestones in other forms such as personified rising suns and winged skulls. The Chandler verse expressed another way might be, "Even though my physical body no longer exists, my soul is still with God." But…skin worms? Those more graphic verses, another example being "my body moulders in the dust," fell out of favor by the end of the century.

THE WOODMAN MONUMENT, WILTON

In the far back corner of the Weld Street Cemetery is the other billboard serving two purposes. In that case, the four granite posts erected around the Woodman family lot are fitted with chains instead of rods. This one also differs from the Chandler monument in that its inscriptions are on the inside of the family lot, while the Chandler inscriptions face outside. The Woodman billboard is quite large, too. At over six feet wide and two feet tall, it weighs 365 pounds.

The post-and-chain fenced lot of Ephraim Woodman's family in Wilton.

The Woodman marble slab is fit into pocket-slot posts that are level and sound. However, the two posts at the opposite end of the lot have fallen, so the chains no longer serve as intended. This monument is special for another reason—it was signed by its maker and gives us one more name to add to the list of those who created these interesting monuments.

ELIZABETH AND FLORENCE WOODMAN

Ephraim W. Woodman was born in Wilton in 1822, one of nine siblings and the second son named Ephraim (his brother was born and died in 1818, and both were namesakes of their father). He married Elizabeth Fenderson of Wilton in 1846. He must have had some links to the Boston area, since the vital record of their marriage is from that city and notes that he was at that time "of Boston." Later, in the 1860 census, he was living in Cambridge.

The 1850 census for Wilton has Ephraim, Elizabeth, and their one-year-old daughter Florence living in a large household consisting of two brothers (Odlin Watson, a chair maker, and Leonard Watson, a cabinetmaker, along with their families and one other unrelated chair maker). While the three other adult men in the house all had furniture-making occupations, Ephraim's occupation was listed as "none." Despite not working at the time, he had real estate holdings valued at $2,000, more than all the others in the household combined.

Florence died shortly after the census was recorded in 1850, at the age of 2. There's a small square stone laid over her grave in the family lot that reads "CHILD," but her name was inscribed on the billboard. Her mother Elizabeth died in 1851 at the age of 21.

The monument has three panels, but only the center was used, listing Elizabeth and Florence. Ephraim must have intended to have the first panel for himself, and perhaps the third for future family members. He was still in his 20s when he lost his wife and daughter, and surely planned to one day remarry and start again.

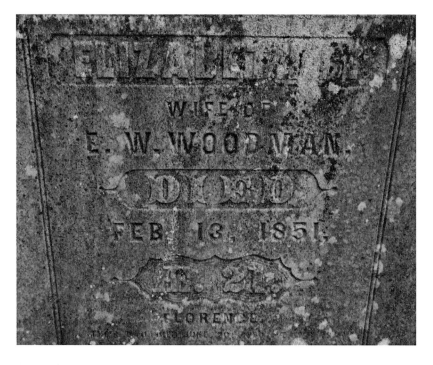

Above: The center panel of the Woodman monument, the only one inscribed on this billboard.

Left: Civil War portrait of Ephraim Woodman from the Maine State Archives.

The years that followed brought Ephraim to Minnesota (1859), where he purchased 40 acres of land near his brother Isaac's property. There, he received another 120 acres of land from the government as part of a land grant act that deeded land to servicemen. He then returned to Massachusetts (1860) and married Sarah Elizabeth Hiscock. He entered the military for the Union during the Civil War; his photograph in uniform is in the collections of the Maine State Archives. Throughout the 1860s, various records have him back in Maine, in Wisconsin (location of the birth of his son), and in Mississippi (location of the birth of another son). It was in Mississippi where, in 1869, Ephraim's appendix ruptured, causing his death at the age of 46. Neither his name, nor that of his second family, appears on the Weld Street Cemetery billboard.

MONUMENT MAKER: RICHARD SMITH

When I visited the Woodman billboard, I measured it, inspected it to assess its health, and took photographs for use in the book. It wasn't until I was home looking at the pictures that I noticed an eroded signature in the lower right corner. Zooming in got me partway there—I could read "R. Smith" and one other word that I expected to be a town name (as commonly done by midcentury marble workers). I was thrilled! I had already tentatively assigned this monument to Richard Smith, based on a gravestone he'd signed at Portland's Eastern Cemetery.[19] On both, his carving of the word "DIED" matched and was quite distinctive, using lettering identified by my friend Lynne Baggett as "exaggerated bifurcated serif." So, I now had record of three makers of billboard monuments.

Richard Smith was one of the many marble workers operating in southern Maine in the midcentury. He was born in 1818 and grew

---

19. That marker is a white marble tablet stone dated 1847 for Catherine Mitchell; it had been broken for a while, but was repaired by the Spirits Alive conservationists in 2018.

up in Bridgton. The 1850 census listed him in Portland with his wife, two daughters, and an apprentice stonecutter named George Leavitt. At that time, Richard was in partnership with Benjamin Chaney; their business—Smith & Chaney—was at 308 Congress Street. The

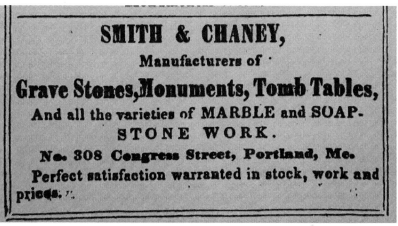

SMITH & CHANEY,
Manufacturers of ·
Grave Stones, Monuments, Tomb Tables,
And all the varieties of MARBLE and SOAP-STONE WORK.

No. 308 Congress Street, Portland, Me.
Perfect satisfaction warranted in stock, work and prices.

1850 advertisement for Richard Smith and Benjamin Chaney's shop in Portland.

partnership didn't last more than a couple of years. According to the 1853 directory, Richard was no longer in Portland and the stonecutting shop at 308 Congress was then occupied by the firm of Hunt & Jewett, the makers of the Hill family billboard in Yarmouth (Chapter 6). By 1856, Richard was living in Bridgton again, as his name appeared in the *Maine Register and Business Directory* as a marble worker that year. Then, in the 1860 census, Richard was in Dixfield, 50 miles north of Bridgton.

In order to narrow down a production date for this monument, I needed to know what town Richard Smith listed next to his name. I just couldn't make it out from my pictures, so I asked for help on the MOCA Facebook page, wondering if there was anyone who lived near Wilton who could visit the stone and get a better shot of the signature. Sam Howes came to the rescue! Within a couple of days, Sam visited the cemetery and sent me a good photo of the signature. The town name was clear—Dixfield. Given Smith's whereabouts, I assigned production of this monument to the late 1850s, with my thanks to Sam for his help.

As he got older, Richard Smith left the business of marble work behind. He and his family moved to Haverhill, Massachusetts, where he became a shoemaker in one of the mills. By 1880 he was a widower and boarding with someone else. He married a third time late in life and died of acute dysentery in 1889 at the age of 71. Though he died in Haverhill, his remains were brought home to Maine, where there is a record of burial in Bridgton at the High Street Cemetery.

CHAPTER 14

LIEUTENANT BUTTERFIELD AND DOCTOR THING

THE BUTTERFIELD MONUMENT, WILTON

*W*ilton is a billboard hotspot. More of these monuments are found there than in any other town in Maine. Three are at the Weld Street Cemetery and two are located at the East Wilton Cemetery, one of which is the next to be examined. It's a stocky little billboard just over three feet wide and 18 inches tall. It has a thicker-cut slab than most, which bumps its weight up to 160 pounds. The granite posts are overly large, and the slab is pinned to the posts in the same manner as the Chandler monument covered in the last chapter. I believe this to be one of the backdated monuments—it's clearly contemporary to the billboards made in the 1850s and 1860s, but I've not narrowed it down any further than that.

Lieutenant Isaac Butterfield was born 1773 in Dunstable, Massachusetts. Polly Pease was born on Martha's Vineyard in 1776. Those who are paying careful attention to the genealogical details of the families covered thus far should have bells ringing in their heads. There was another woman named Pease from Martha's Vineyard memorialized on a billboard: Love Pease Chandler, born 1763. A coincidence that they're both on billboards? Perhaps. But

The Butterfield billboard at the East Wilton Cemetery. Note the biocidal cleaning effect running beneath the bronze bolts.

the cemeteries where they rest are less than two miles apart as the crow flies.

Isaac gained his rank of lieutenant during his service in the War of 1812, yet interestingly, he is known to have joined the Wilton Defense in 1814. That group was described in the newspaper at the time as "A large number of gentlemen exempt by law from military duty, have become organized and partly equipped, for the purpose of guarding, protecting, and vindicating their rights, in case of foreign invasion." He was just over 40 at the time, so perhaps his exemption from duty was age-related. He died in May of 1816 of typhus fever, after a "tedious sickness." In the newspaper notice of his death, he was listed as a captain, not a lieutenant. The newspaper went on further to note that "This fever has prevailed very extensively in the town of Wilton since the 1st of last March, and proved mortal in about 14 cases during that time."

Polly Pease died in 1829 at the age of 56. They'd had five children, all but one of whom reached adulthood. The single exception was for middle child Isaac Jr., who died in 1817 at age 11. A single line running along the bottom of the marble billboard memorializes him.

Dennis Montagna, with whom I serve on the AGS board of directors, made what he called an admittedly geeky observation about this billboard: "With bronze bolts screwed into ferrous nuts, you get a bio-cidal cleaning effect on the marble billboard and iron staining on the granite supports behind."

The reverse side of the Butterfield monument. Note the rusty staining running down the granite posts.

THE THING MONUMENT, MOUNT VERNON

Ira Thing was born in Mount Vernon, Maine, in 1808. As a young man, he owned his first grocery store in Hallowell. He sold it in 1834 and moved back to his hometown for the rest of his life. His first marriage to Lucinda Corey was short-lived; she died in 1837 only 18 months after their wedding. He married again the next year, to Martha

Ann Russ (formerly Rust, according to a Rust family genealogy). They had a son whom they named Everard Russ Thing; he later legally changed his name to Everard Russ, dropping Thing as a surname. Ira attended Harvard Medical School from 1843 to 1845 and it was after his return to Mount Vernon that he began to refer to himself as "Dr. Thing." During his time at Harvard, Martha Ann died. She was 26.

The monument for Dr. Thing and his two wives at Stevens Cemetery. Note the empty photo pocket.

Dr. Thing married for the third time in 1849. His new wife was Sarah E. Robinson, and she brought her infant son Elbridge M. Robinson into the family. The 1850 census for Mount Vernon confirms the family at that time: Dr. Thing, a physician (age 41), wife, Sarah (28), son Everard (8), and step-son Elbridge Robinson (4). That decade is rich with information about Dr. Thing, as he frequently placed notices and advertisements in the *Maine Farmer* newspaper. He advertised himself as an "Eclectic Physician," dealing in botanical medicines. As a justice of the peace for the town, he married quite a few couples.

He seems to have had some difficulty settling on an occupation, wavering between running a general goods store, being a physician, and being a pharmacist. In December 1851 he advertised his new fully stocked village general store, naming dozens of grocery and dry goods items for sale, along with apparel, tools, paints, and 25 medicines. It read, "Dr. T. also keeps an assortment of good Liquors and Wines to use in his Practice…but *not* to be used as a beverage." It was, after all, the period of prohibition in Maine. Just one month later, in January of 1852, he placed a notice that he had disposed of his store's stock and trade, stating he would "for the future give exclusive attention to the PRACTICE of MEDICINE, and will be ready at all times to attend to the calls of suffering." Then in 1853, he returned to selling drugs and medicines at his Agency Store in the village.

In 1857 he had another "contemplated change in my business" when he announced he was going to—once again—sell groceries, dry goods, and supplies in his store. He noted that "MRS. S. E. THING is constantly supplied with a good assortment of MILLINERY GOODS and DRESS TRIMMINGS, which she will always sell at fair prices." In 1858 he ran an ad entitled "Flour. Flour. Flour.," in which he announced a special sale on…well…flour!

A fifth switchback came in October 1859, when he announced he would exclusively practice medicine because he had sold the stock of his store to George McGaffey. It should come as no surprise that just six months later, in April 1860, Dr. Thing placed a notice in the newspaper that he had taken back "the store recently occupied by George McGaffey." But he wasn't giving up medicine this time, promising to be available to treat ailing people at his home or theirs.

Dr. Thing wrote his last will and testament in April of 1865, noting that he was "sound of mind and memory but weak and infirm of body." He listed a series of desires, the first three of which were:

1st. I desire to be buried in the family burial ground near Edwin Stevens.

2nd. I desire that my former wives, Lucinda Cory and Martha Ann be disinterred and removed to the aforesaid family burying ground.

3rd. I desire that suitable headstones be placed over their graves.

Dr. Thing named his brother, Samuel Thing of Freeport, to be his executor. He instructed Samuel to provide $300 to his son Everard and $300 to the "son of my present wife" (Elbridge, Sarah's boy) with the balance of the estate going to Sarah. He died the next month and in the fall of 1865 his house and land were sold at an estate sale.

In the probate file for Dr. Thing, I found that $70 was paid on June 12, 1866, to William H. Rollins for a gravestone. That one line in the estate's settlement of expenses confirmed three important details about billboard monuments: production date, cost, and a fourth monument maker.

MONUMENT MAKER: WILLIAM H. ROLLINS

I lost track of Sarah Thing after Ira died. No vital records of remarriage or death have been found for her. But what's clear is that her name would not appear on the billboard monument erected by Samuel Thing for his brother Ira and Ira's first two wives. When stonecutter William Rollins created the monument in 1866 he divided the inscription surface into three panels. There was no room for the doctor's third wife, Sarah. Recall that in his will, Dr. Thing had desired "suitable headstones" (note the plural) be placed over their graves. It seems that his brother Samuel decided a single monument for all of them would suffice.

The Thing billboard is found at the Stevens Cemetery in Mount Vernon. It's one of the pocket-slot granite post types. The whole structure is dangerously tilting, perhaps 30 degrees. This billboard is fitted with a metal rod between the posts so if it falls, it will likely all go down in one piece. When I visited Stevens Cemetery it was a conservation site with many markers in the midst of being cleaned and repaired. My gravestone friend Deb Probert told me that Bob Grenier had worked on at least four dozen markers by the time I visited. Hopefully someday the Thing billboard can be set back upright too.

On the stone, second wife Martha is listed first, first wife Lucinda is listed second, and the doctor occupies the third panel. Over his

The Thing monument leans heavily backward and is in some danger of falling or breaking.

name is an empty photograph pocket. The slab is just under five feet wide, but its unusual thickness of three inches makes this a heavy one at 350 pounds.

William H. Rollins's name appears among the many other marble workers in the 1856 *Maine Business Directory.* He lived in Standish at that time. I don't know a lot about him, except that he was born in New Hampshire in 1814 and his wife, Mary, was about the same age. They had one son (William Jr.) and a daughter Martha, who I believe was Mary's child from a previous marriage. In the 1860 census they were living in Standish; his namesake son had passed away already but their daughter Martha was 11. Also in the house were two kids with the surname Davis whose relationship to William is unclear. Eldra Davis was 9 and Pitt Davis was 8 (he was listed as being blind). In 1870, just William and Mary were living together in the town of Wayne, and he had by then switched from stone work to cabinetry. He was 55. Daughter Martha died in 1871.

A GRAVESTONE MAKER TO THE VERY END

Though general details about him are sparse, I found his probate file from 1873 to be most interesting. William, certainly familiar with gravestones and their making, gave very specific instructions as to the monument to be placed on his own grave, as follows:

> I hereby direct my Executor to place at the head of my grave and my wife and adopted daughter a granite base eight feet long, eighteen inches wide, and twelve inches thick, hammered on the face and each thereon three monuments, for myself, wife, and adopted daughter. Those for myself and my wife to be twenty inches square and eight inches thick, with a plinth six inches thick projecting one and one half inches—the one for my adopted daughter to be eighteen inches square, eight inches thick, with plinth as above, all of best Italian marble suitably inscribed. It is my wish that the name and age of deceased son William H. Rollins Jr. be inscribed upon the monument of my deceased adopted daughter.

It appears that his wishes were fulfilled fairly closely, as there are three stones for the family resting on a long granite base at Mount Pleasant Cemetery in Wayne.

William further directed his executor to divide the remainder of his estate equally between his brother and sister. His sister's name? Mrs. Mary Ann Rust. I'd be willing to bet that there is a familial connection between William's sister Mary Ann Rust and Dr. Thing's second wife, Martha Ann Russ/Rust, but there are more billboards to explore in the next chapter...

CHAPTER 15

THREE COUPLES FROM WELLS

*T*his chapter examines billboards from Wells and Ogunquit that memorialize three couples. Of the 150 names found on Maine's 38 billboards, these three men and three women are of the earliest generation; none was born later than 1751. Though each couple had many children, their monuments were created only for them.

THE MAXWELL MONUMENT, OGUNQUIT

The seaside town of Ogunquit was a village of Wells in its early days, so historic records often use Wells instead of Ogunquit. Alexander Maxwell was born in Wells in 1748; Philadelphia Rankin[20] was born there in 1751. They were married in 1772 and had at least 11 children over a 22-year period. Alexander served in the American Revolution

---

20. Recall her relationship to the Hill children on the monument at Ocean View Cemetery in Wells, covered in Chapter 4.

and was a member of the Wells Committee of Correspondence.[21] He appeared in the first census taken in the United States in 1790 as a 42-year-old head of household consisting of eight.

In 1812, he and his neighbors along the south coast road petitioned the justices of the Court of Common Pleas in York for road improvements. The petition read, "That the Highway or common road, leading from York lower Meeting house to the house of Alexander Maxwell in Wells, is in many places so narrow, crooked and bad, that at some seasons of the year it is quite impassable, and at all seasons rough, inconvenient and even dangerous to travelers." What would he think if he could see the paved road that connects the towns today?

Alexander must have traveled that road many, many times, as he lived to age 94. Philadelphia had died 22 years before him; she passed in 1821, he passed in 1843. In his death notice published in the *Portland Weekly Advertiser*, Alexander Maxwell was remembered as a religious man who was fond of reading. He studied the Bible and was delighted to share his extensive knowledge of it with others. He died of an unspecified illness, described only as "lingering and painful." And when he died he left seven children, 42 grandchildren, and 16 great-grandchildren.

The monument is a white marble stone of the pocket-slot variety. The slab is just over three feet wide and 15 inches tall, though a close look at the post slots shows that the stonecutter planned for a slab measuring 17 or 18 inches in height. There is a metal rod holding the two granite posts together, but it's in an unusual position—above the slab. Most were installed below the inscription slab.

When I first saw this monument, it was slipping from one post just a bit due to the posts splaying slightly. In the fall of 2019, after my presentation at the annual meeting of the Maine Cemetery Association,[22]

---

21. This committee was formed to communicate with the government and with neighboring towns as the need arose to address matters of common interest, such as safety and the protection of the townspeople.

22. This is the group of cemetery directors and not to be confused with MOCA, the Maine Old Cemetery Association.

The Maxwell billboard in Ogunquit.

Sonny Perkins introduced himself to me. He's a caretaker at the Riverside Cemetery in Ogunquit, where the Maxwell monument is, and he told me that he'd recently done some conservation work there, including resetting the billboard. We decided to meet at the cemetery soon after and I was able to see firsthand the fine work he's done. Sonny reset the posts and fit the slab back into place. It's now looking as good as new, thanks to Sonny's efforts.

THE STAPLES MONUMENT, WELLS

The names of the second couple, John and Tabitha Staples, are found on a small drop-slot billboard near the front of Ocean View Cemetery. They were born in 1733 and 1743, respectively, and married in Wells in 1762. Vital records aren't clear, but an unsourced family tree on ancestry.com lists eight children born to them from 1765 to 1786.

In 1767, a new First Parish Meeting House was built in Wells. The pews were divided into ranks, with the lower floor pews near the front being valued more highly than those in the back and the pews in the upstairs gallery being valued less than the pews on the floor. A committee was designated to assign the 56 men (heads of households) who were members of the church to ranks. Instead of considering net worth, taxes paid, or some other logical consideration, the committee made decisions by considering each man's perceived importance to the community. The first rank included 14 men; they were able to select the best-located pews on the floor. The second rank consisted of 25, who were able to select their pews from the ones on the floor left unclaimed by the more fortunate first rank. John Staples was not among those first two ranks. The remaining 17 men were divided into two final ranks for the selection of their pews upstairs in the gallery. Among the 11 listed in the third rank was John Staples.

In 1780, some communities had difficulty recruiting soldiers to serve in the military. John was part of a local committee formed to help determine the terms of payment for soldiers who might be enticed into enlisting for three years of service.

In the first census for the United States in 1790, John was listed as head of a household consisting of three males and seven females. In 1800, it was just John and Tabitha plus three kids. Tabitha died in 1802 at age 59; John followed ten years later, passing at the age of 79.

The billboard erected for them is another small one; at just three feet long and 16 inches tall, it weighs about 100 pounds. There is a metal crossbar in the more traditional position—below the slab—yet there is a full break in the lower left corner of the monument.

The Staples billboard in Wells.

THE HUBBARD MONUMENT, WELLS

Deeper into the same cemetery is the final billboard in this trio. It's for Joseph Hubbard, born 1741, and Ann Gowan (sometimes Anna and sometimes Gowen) Hubbard, born 1750. A line is inscribed along the bottom of the slab that reads, "They were both born in the town of Kittery, ME." The Hubbards had four sons and five daughters.

Joseph was a tanner and well-known in Wells. During the American Revolution, Joseph became a colonel in the local military regiment, and in the *History of Wells and Kennebunk* there's an interesting account of an incident that occurred on his first day on the job.

> One of his soldiers came to salute him on the morning when he first invested himself with his regimentals. As the colonel came to the door, the private raised his gun in the usual way of salutation, and (accidentally) fired. The charge entered a puddle of filth made by the sink-spout, and completely besmeared the new buff breaches of the superior, then a material part of his official wardrobe. Dr. Hemmenway told Hubbard that he thought it would have frightened him somewhat; but Hubbard replied that he would have stood his ground if it had blown him into the sky. The salutation was not very gratifying in its results, but Hubbard had accepted it as an intention to honor him in his new position.

He served with Alexander Maxwell on the Committee of Correspondence, so Hubbard and Maxwell were certainly well acquainted. I suspect that they knew John Staples too; Hubbard served in the same capacity as Staples on the local committee established to help determine payment standards to entice men to serve in the military. Ann died in 1796 at age 46, and Joseph remarried the following year. His new wife was the already twice-married Alice Wheelwright. Within a year of their marriage there was trouble, leading to Joseph running this notice in the newspaper:

Whereas Alice, wife of me the subscriber, has escaped from my bed and board, and has behaved herself in a very unbecoming manner, this therefore is to forbid all persons harboring or trusting her on my account, as I will not pay one cent of her contracting after this date. Joseph Hubbard. Wells, Oct. 25, 1798.

I don't know what happened to the couple as a result of that notice but do know that following Joseph's death Alice married for a fourth time.

The Hubbard billboard in Wells.

He died in 1819 at the age of 78.

This billboard is one of the drop-slot granite post versions, with a metal rod running well below the slab very close to the ground. The marble rests high in the slots and has a small decoration carved at the top center. Like the other two in this chapter, it's just over three feet wide and weighs about 100 pounds. Overall, except for significant powdery lichen growth on the surface, the slab is in good condition.

CHAPTER 16

TWO MORE MONUMENT MAKERS

THE SMITH MONUMENT, WILTON

John Hopley Smith and Sophia (Bean) Smith were born in Readfield, Maine, and married there in 1815. Six daughters and a son were born to them between 1817 and 1833. The family appears in the 1830 census in Chesterville, though a published genealogy for the Bean family strays a bit in noting that all children were born in nearby Wilton. I found little else about John but know that he died at age 49 in 1837. Sophia died over 20 years later at the age of 69, according to the official town and county records. She'd been ill for 15 months with consumption before her death in October of 1859. The Bean genealogy strays here too, reporting her death a year earlier. The year of death inscribed on the billboard matches the official records, so we'll go with that. But the carver etched her age as 56 instead of 65, way off the official record. If we are to believe him, she would have been married when she was 12. And if we are to believe the genealogy, she delivered her first child five months after marriage (that's *possible*, but given a few other mismatches I tend to think the genealogy is inaccurate with regard to her details).

Notwithstanding the inconsistencies regarding Sophia's dates and age, the billboard that bears her name is located at the East Wilton

The reverse side of the Smith monument at East Wilton Cemetery.

Cemetery. It is of the pocket-slot granite post variety, the posts of which were created with pyramidal tops. The slab is over four feet by two feet and weighs at least 225 pounds. There's no metal crossbar on this monument. In general, it appears upright and sound, though a small stress fracture is found on the lower edge of the marble.

Unlike most others, this billboard was not divided into inscription panels. Instead, the names of husband and wife were centered on the stone and surrounded with decorative elements. It does not appear that there was ever an intent to add other names to this gravestone. The carver used four different lettering types on the inscription, perhaps as a means to advertise his ability with the chisel.

MONUMENT MAKER: GEORGE W. WISE

On the lower right of the slab we find a signature, "G. Wise, Canton." This is a new name for our list of makers and the fifth man known to

Detail of the Smith billboard showing the signature of George Wise.

Detail of the Smith billboard showing George Wise's decorative leafy twig. Also note the small stress fracture just below the design.

have produced billboards. I have assigned a production date of 1860, and George W. Wise was indeed a marble worker living in Canton, according to the 1860 census. He was 29 at the time, married to his first wife, Eleanor A. Keith (sometimes Elenor or Elanor). They had two toddlers then, a boy, Frank, and a girl, Ella; then one more boy named George was born in 1861. Frank outlived his siblings and owned a clothing business. His younger brother George was lost at sea.

At the outset of the Civil War, George served as a private in the Twenty-sixth Maine Infantry. Eleanor died in 1864 and George remarried 1867. His second wife was ten years younger than he; she was Arvilla (sometimes Orvilla) Rolfe, and they had one son together. Following George through the census records, we find him moving around Maine from Canton (1860) to Rumford (1870) to Paris (1880 and 1900), and a marble worker for at least those 40 years. George seems to have operated on his own terms. He did not join the Maine Charitable Mechanic Association nor was he listed in the *Maine Business Directory* as a marble worker. I found no advertisements for a stone-cutting business in his name—just a single line at the end of a column entitled "East Rumford" in the *Oxford Democrat* published May 7, 1869, which read, "Mr. George Wise has opened a very nice marble shop at the Falls."

Kidney disease caused George's death in 1913. He was buried at the Mount Auburn Cemetery in Norway, and his grave is marked with a stone shared with his first wife Eleanor.

The Goodwin Monument, Ripley

One September day in 2019, a nice lady from the town of Ripley returned my desperate call, cautioning me that the Downing Cemetery would not be easy to find: "You can't see it from the road. Drive back toward Dexter and look on the left for a narrow path into the woods along the side of the road." I'd been unable to pinpoint the cemetery using Google Earth, the MOCA website, findagrave.com, and a paper map; thus my cry for help to the town. Despite receiving directions from the nice lady and having a second set of eyes (my spouse, who is always very good at following directions), I never found it. And so, the Goodwin billboard is the only one of the 38 in Maine that I have not personally "met."

However, I did find a second grave marker for the young woman memorialized on that well-hidden billboard. She was Lydia P. Goodwin, age 42, and there is a fairly standard-looking marble tablet gravestone for her at the Mount Pleasant Cemetery in Dexter. She died in 1856. Her husband was buried there too, with a matching

Above: Not only is Downing Cemetery hard to find, the bill-board monument within it is well hidden by ferns. Photo courtesy of Wynona Randall.

Left: This is the second grave-stone for Lydia Goodwin, which is found in Dexter immediately next to an identical stone for her husband.

marker in his name: Nathaniel Goodwin, 1862. I suspect that when Nathaniel died the family decided to disinter Lydia's remains and move them to be with her husband—in the much more easily found cemetery in Dexter.

The billboard that was first erected for Lydia was made in 1856. Her ten-week-old daughter, who had died less than a month before her, is on the billboard as well, but unnamed. No stone for the infant is found near the markers for her parents five miles east in Dexter, suggesting that her remains were not moved along with her mother's after Nathaniel died in 1862 (but if not, why not?).

Nathaniel Goodwin was a shoemaker. He and Lydia married in 1844. Two daughters were born to them prior to the unnamed infant in 1855. After Lydia passed, Nathaniel did marry again, but within a few years he died as well.

The billboard monument is of the pocket-slot granite post variety. There is a metal crossbar running along the top of the monument and there appears to be a small stress fracture in the upper right corner of the slab. While I have not been able to measure the marble on my own, I know that it is four feet wide by two feet tall. How? Because the original order form for this monument exists in the records of its maker: Baker, Emery & Co. of Skowhegan.

Monument Makers: Baker, Emery & Co.

Over the course of my 2019 research I posted frequently on the MOCA Facebook page, reporting newly found billboards, posting pictures, and asking for help finding more. After one such update Steve Dow sent a note that he'd found Lydia and her infant listed in the *Marble Records Index*. Cheryl Willis Patten then supplied background information about this source, as she had done much of the cataloging work in 2006 before turning this valuable resource over to the Maine Historical Society for its collections.

Thanks to Steve and Cheryl, I visited the MHS and spent a few hours poring over the dozens of original order books created by the men who worked at the Skowhegan marble company. The original record of this billboard as ordered by Nathaniel Goodwin in 1856 is in *Book No. 1, April 16, 1855 to November 10, 1856,* under the company name of *Baker, Emery & Co.*

Harrison D. Baker and Charles C. Emery were actually the second owners of the business. The company began in 1846. Baker and Emery purchased it in 1853. Charles Emery sold his interest in 1863, and Harrison Baker continued the firm with John Judkins for many more years. A helpful chronological history found in the *Marble Records Index* is worth reading in its entirety, but for the purposes of this book readers should know that the company was in operation for over 100 years under a succession of at least five owners.

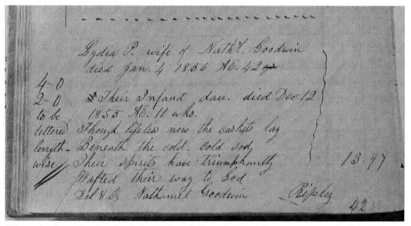

The order form for the Goodwin billboard from the Skowhegan company Baker, Emery & Co. Source: Maine Historical Society.

The order confirms the size of the slab. Note the left margin shows four feet by two feet "to be lettered lengthwise." At the bottom we find "Del & Cg" (assumed to be delivered to and charged by) then the name Nathaniel Goodwin. And in the right margin the price was listed as $13.97. The inscription details and epitaph are reproduced here exactly as written in the order book, since the writing in the book has faded over the years:

Lydia P. wife of Nath'l Goodwin
died Jan. 4 1856 AE 42 ys.
Their infant dau. died Dec 12
1855 AE 10 weeks
Though lifeless now the caskets lay
Beneath the cold, cold sod
Their spirits have triumphantly
Wafted their way to God

While I was sad to have not been able to actually find the Goodwin billboard, any tears were quickly dried by my glee at being able to add a sixth monument maker, another confirmed production date, and another billboard cost to my growing base of knowledge about these monuments.

CHAPTER 17

MASSIVE YET FRAGILE

I chose the final three Maine monuments for this chapter so that I could illustrate how billboards, while massive, can be quite fragile. Most slabs are marble and therefore subject to the same slow deterioration found on traditional marble gravestones. Weather is their enemy! Rain saturates the relatively porous stone, and if it freezes, minute ice crystals form within and may microburst the surrounding stone as they expand. Over time, the gravestone "sugars" into fine granules that slough off the base stone, making inscriptions and designs more blurry or eroded. Additionally, lichen takes hold, the ground shifts, mowers bump into monuments, and vandals lurk in the shadows.

On top of all this, the very design of billboard monuments seems to threaten failure—they're heavy pieces of stone held up in the air! The stone's weight exerts a great deal of downward pressure on support structures. Posts crack or break or get pushed apart by the gravitational weight of the stone. Some slabs that are still seemingly held securely within their supports exhibit stress cracks, especially found along the bottom edges. These may later expand into full breaks.

THE WARREN MONUMENT, JACKSON

The billboard memorializing Reverend Silas Warren and his wife Abigail (Smith) Warren is located at the Jackson Corner Cemetery. Silas was Harvard-educated. He and Abigail married in 1799 and had at least four children. They moved to Maine around 1810, where Silas initially served as a field missionary. Having made good connections in the towns of Brooks and Jackson, he was ordained as minister there in 1812. He remained very active in Jackson throughout his life, serving as schoolmaster and state representative in addition to preaching. In his 1856 obituary, he was described as a cheerful, calm, and dignified man. It noted, "He had long looked forward to death as a happy release, and at last he sank quietly away as in sleep. It was the natural, peaceful close of a venerable old age." Abigail outlived her husband by just a year. She passed at the age of 82 in 1857.

The Warren billboard in Jackson, slipping from its posts and slightly askew.

The monument is of the drop-slot granite post variety; it's one of those with posts having very short slots in it, so the stone stands quite tall in its frame. The posts have begun to splay a bit, whether due to the weight of the slab or the shifting of ground due to freeze/thaw cycles that occur during Maine's early spring and late fall. The slab weighs about 250 pounds. It is slipping from the left post and therefore no longer level. The metal rod connecting the granite posts may prevent the posts from further splaying, so the slab could remain in this skewed position for some time. Still, the threat exists that it could slip out of the posts altogether.

THE BURNHAM MONUMENT, GARLAND

Kimberly J. Sawtelle found this next billboard for me at the Burnham Cemetery while she was roaming around Garland one summer day in 2019. It has a unique design consisting of partially slotted granite posts and metal tabs. The posts have very short slots that hold the marble slab in place, assisted by a short, centrally positioned third slotted post that may not be original to the monument (the slab does not perfectly fit within it). Closer to the top of the slab there are metal tabs that prevent the inscribed stone from leaning forward or backward.

The impressive Burnham billboard at Garland's Burnham Cemetery.

Detail of the Burnham billboard, showing the stabilizing metal tabs near the tops of the posts.

The posts are very tall and finished with pyramidal caps. The slab has five panels, each dedicated to one member of the Burnham family. The marble measures six and a half feet long, two feet tall, and weighs 350 pounds. The whole structure sits on a large base stone, elevating it higher off the ground than all others and giving it a grand feel.

The billboard memorializes Eleazer Burnham, his two wives (Mary and Matilda), his only son Charles, and his eldest daughter Matilda. I've assigned a production date of 1863 as I believe that Eleazer had it made for his wives and children, who had all died by that year. Their inscriptions are on the first four panels and seem to be in the same hand and style. Under each of their names is a unique verse. One example for his wife Mary is: *"Was it my heavenly Father's will, To call her home so soon? Then I will love that Father still, And her beyond the tomb."* For his young daughter Matilda we find: *"Come little children unto me, Direct then not to stay. Then in my father's house shall be, Bright stars through endless day."* Eleazer died in 1888; the inscription for him is on the fifth (final) panel and has less depth to the lettering than the others. Additionally, there is no verse inscribed below his name. I believe his name was added some 25 years after the monument was erected.

The back of the Burnham billboard monument.

Detail of the Burnham billboard, showing one of the severely cracked posts.

The reason for including this impressive monument in this chapter is that the posts are in very poor condition. The bottom of each is severely cracked and both have been encircled with metal braces meant to hold the pieces together. The danger for this monument is, of course, that if the posts were to crumble and fail completely the entire monument would fall. It's one of the most threatened in the Maine collection.

One other monument in the Burnham Cemetery is a "must see" stone. It's for Eleazer's son-in-law Lyman E. Richardson. Around the time this young man enlisted for service in the Civil War, he married Eleazer's daughter Mary, who is not listed on the Burnham billboard. He was a schoolteacher in Garland; she was described in Oak's *History of Garland* as "an intelligent lady of Garland." He died in August of

1861 from injuries he'd received during the Battle of Bull Run a month earlier. His leg had been mostly torn off by a cannonball during the fighting. He survived long enough to persevere through the surgery necessary to fully amputate his leg (said to have been done without chloroform), but died soon after. Though many of the men lost in that battle were buried in Virginia where they fell, Eleazer Burnham made persistent—and ultimately successful—efforts to bring Lyman's remains back to Maine for burial. The monument that honors him is within view of the Burnham billboard and has a wonderful full figure of a soldier carved onto a large marble obelisk.

The Adams Monument, Wilton

The final billboard is found at Weld Street in Wilton. It's for the young family of Charles M. Adams. He, too, served in the Civil War, but he died on his way home in 1862. Charles Morris Adams was a twin; he and his brother John Mosher Adams were born in 1836. Charles married Betsey Ann Cheney in May of 1857; that November she gave birth to their first and only child, Fred Morris Adams. Fred died before reaching age 2 in 1859. Charles and Betsey were on their own in the 1860 census; he was a shoemaker.

The Adams billboard's inscribed marble slab.

In 1861, the twins, along with their older brothers Isaac and Joshua, enlisted for service in the Eighth Maine Regiment. Charles was a drummer; his rank was "musician" and his war record indicates he served as field staff in the band. Another brother named George—who was younger than these four—also enlisted but was not accepted into service. Still, he accompanied his older brother John into war as his helper. The Eighth Maine was organized in Augusta and mustered into service for a three-year enlistment in the fall of 1861. It was originally attached to General Sherman's South Carolina Expeditionary Corps and remained in the Hilton Head and Beaufort areas for most of the members' service. The regiment lost 381 men: six officers and 128 enlisted men were killed or mortally wounded; four officers and 243 enlisted men died of disease.

While Charles was serving in the South, his wife died back home in Maine. Betsey was just 26 when she passed in February of 1862. Around that time, Charles was discharged from service due to disability. On his way home, he died in New York City (cause of death being listed as chronic diarrhea). Despite a concerted effort, I have not been able to discover if he was buried in New York or back home in Wilton.

The back side of the Adams billboard.

144

The monument is included in this chapter because it has completely fallen from its posts. It's not a particularly large billboard. The marble piece is four feet wide and 20 inches tall, weighing 175 pounds, and since it was set relatively low to the ground it did not break when it fell. It appears that the posts, which do not have a metal crossbar between them, splayed enough for the slab to just drop to the ground. The slab itself appears sound, so if the posts were reset, this monument could be restored nearly to its original appearance.

These three illustrate the range of damage found on Maine's billboards, from simple shifting in place to completely falling from posts. Chapter 20 includes summary information about the full collection of billboards, while the Appendix details specific condition issues for each one.

The posts of the Adams billboard have splayed and the stone has completely fallen from place.

CHAPTER 18

ONE IN A MILLION

*T*hose planning a visit to the South Buxton Cemetery to see the Elden and Lane billboards are encouraged to also allow time for a side trip to the Martin-Titcomb-Elwell Cemetery. It's located about five miles away, hugging the left side of Long Plains Road when heading north. The small multi-family cemetery has just 40 known graves but contains one extraordinary family monument that's related to the billboards.

The remarkable spinning monument for the Elwell family of Buxton.

One of the eight inscription surfaces on the marble piece of the Elwell monument.

It is a large, eight-sided piece of white marble, drilled through and mounted on an axle of sorts. Like billboard monuments, it's held aloft on granite posts. In effect, the monument has eight inscription panels. Benjamin Elwell (1765–1846), his wife, at least five of their children, and in-laws—13 people in all—are memorialized. It was likely produced soon after Elwell's death and, therefore, contemporaneously with the billboards. As installed, it would have allowed a visitor to find a specific individual by spinning the stone; today, the marble piece has been fixed so that it no longer spins (perhaps done as a matter of protection).

A monument with moving parts—just remarkable!

CHAPTER 19

BILLBOARDS OUTSIDE MAINE

*M*aine's billboards received some national attention in the summer of 2019 when I presented a slide show of my research and findings at the annual conference of the Association for Gravestone Studies, held that year at Gardner-Webb University in North Carolina. It was during that presentation that Abby Burnett, from Arkansas, practically jumped out of her chair when I showed pictures of the monuments for the Sargents and Hills. "I know those people!" she exclaimed, and the rest of their story is found in Chapters 5 and 6.

People from all over the country attend AGS conferences and the room was packed that day, so I know gravestone scholars and enthusiasts from many different regions saw the show. When I asked if anyone knew of a billboard monument where they live, there were many heads shaking "no." Previously, Martha Zimicki had found one in Rockingham, Vermont, so I knew there was at least one outside Maine. After the talk I heard from Charlie Marchant and Bob Drinkwater, both with long-time association with the AGS. Bob lives in western Massachusetts and told me he knew of one monument in the town of Montague. Charlie told me he knew of two billboards in Vermont, one in Tunbridge and one in Stowe. Then Dale

The Pulsipher family billboard in Rockingham, Vermont. This one features eight-sided posts.

and Tina Utter got in touch—they'd seen and photographed *two* in Tunbridge at the same cemetery. So the out-of-state list had quickly grown to five.

I was planning a trip to Vermont to see the monuments for myself when MOCA's Jess Couture alerted me that she'd found one near her alma mater in Craftsbury Common, Vermont. That made six. I mapped out a loop drive to see all of those in Vermont and made the trip in the fall. I found and photographed all of them and even got one more on my own in Stowe. That made seven. The day before an AGS board meeting in western Massachusetts in September, Dennis Montagna joined me on a field trip to see the billboard in Montague. So I've officially "met" all seven known (so far) outside Maine.

Obviously, billboards aren't unique to Maine. That seven are found in other New England states suggests this may have been a regional style versus solely created by Maine's marble workers. Still, Maine's collection of 38 is impressive.

The out-of-state billboards share basic design components such as having oblong marble slabs inscribed horizontally, slotted granite

The Putman/Putnam family billboard in Tunbridge, Vermont.

posts, and sometimes metal crossbars for extra support. Slab sizes mirror those found in Maine, generally having widths of four to six feet. However, three of them have posts made of local white marble instead of granite. Today those posts are dark with lichen, but when they were first erected they must have been brilliantly handsome. One other obvious difference is found with the Rockingham billboard: the granite posts are eight-sided instead of the usual four.

The Gunn family billboard in Montague, Massachusetts. This family lot is surrounded on three sides; the billboard and fencing help define its space.

The white marble posts of the Gunn monument must have made for an impressive presentation when newly erected.

I have not done extensive background research on the seven families memorialized on the out-of-state billboards, but provide basic details below for those who wish to see them for themselves.

- Montague, Massachusetts (South Cemetery): Gunn family. Six children are memorialized on a marble slab six feet wide. This monument has white marble slotted posts and is flanked by fencing on two sides, all making a nice boundary to the family lot.
- Craftsbury Common, Vermont (Craftsbury Common Cemetery): Davison family. This monument appears to have its original white marble slab, but a modern support structure. The posts and a unique roof-like capstone running over the slab appear to be replacement pieces more recently made.
- Rockingham, Vermont (Meeting House Cemetery): Pulsipher family. This billboard is the one with the eight-sided slotted granite posts. The monument is in danger of falling, as it is slipping from the posts.

- Stowe, Vermont (Old Yard Cemetery): Bennett family. A husband and wife are memorialized on a marble billboard with marble posts. This is a pocket-slot variety and appears to be in good condition.
- Stowe, Vermont (Old Yard Cemetery): Paine family. Three children are memorialized on a similarly sized marble billboard with marble posts. The posts are cracking, threatening the health of this monument.
- Tunbridge, Vermont (Hutchinson Cemetery): Putnam (or Putman; both versions are used) family. Slotted granite posts hold a marble slab aloft for a wife and three children. Covered in lichen and with cracked posts, this large billboard is in some danger.
- Tunbridge, Vermont (Hutchinson Cemetery): Tyler family. A husband and wife are memorialized on a slab measuring four feet that fits into slotted granite posts. It, too, is in need of a gentle cleaning.

There must be more of these in New England. Hopefully this book will lead to their discovery!

Chapter 20

THE WRAP-UP

I wrote this book to shine a spotlight on a type of monument I've
found to be particularly interesting and that's not been well studied before. During the journey I documented a variety of construction
details and found family stories that touched on a few of the important
social issues in Maine at the time, including prohibition, the Civil War,
abolition, and epidemic illness.

In the first chapter, I pondered a few questions: Who came up with
the idea of the billboard? When were they made? Was there just one
maker? Are they found anywhere else? I'm satisfied that my research
has resulted in answers to the last three: production dates, monument
makers, and a few locations outside Maine are now known. The one
lingering curiosity is the question of origin. As detailed in that chapter,
I think the idea of English roots has merit. But I find it interesting that
there's about a three-generation gap in time between the last-known
American made grave-board (located outside New England) and the
rise of the stone billboards in Maine. Whatever brought them to light
in the mid-1800s will probably remain a mystery, but what's clear is
that once this monument type was introduced it was produced by multiple stonecutters and took many forms.

Studying gravestones is an enjoyable occupation for an old retired guy like me to have. Though I've spent a great deal of time immersing myself in stone details, I do sometimes pause to reflect on the people these monuments were built to honor. All of us have lost someone we dearly love; having lost both of my parents recently I know the grief and sadness of death. But I cannot imagine what it was like for the Traftons to lose five of their six children over the course of a month, or for Mrs. Foss to be left alone to care for her four young children when her husband was lost at sea. All of the billboards have some family tragedies at their very core.

In previous chapters I covered individual details of all 38 billboards in Maine; I end this book with some summary information that creates a big picture view of them.

Co-location: One interesting thing that has emerged is that 22 of the billboards (58 percent of the total) are located in a cemetery where another one exists. In fact, Cumberland, Kennebunkport, Wells, and Wilton each have a cemetery with three billboards. This suggests that families visiting a cemetery with a billboard liked the look of it enough to want one for their own family. With thousands of cemeteries located in Maine, it seems to be just too much of a coincidence for the majority of billboards to be co-located with others.

Counties: Billboards are found in ten of 16 Maine counties in the south and west of the state. Yet despite a lot of searching, I've not found any in the small adjoining coastal counties of Sagadahoc, Lincoln, and Knox. They *should* have billboards; the counties that surround them all do and the towns within them have plenty of cemeteries filled with other midcentury gravestone forms.

Production dates: Billboards were clearly a midcentury thing. There are four confirmed dates of 1853, 1856, 1859 and 1866, two from the stones themselves, one from probate, and one from a business order. Based on a variety of factors, I've assigned ten others to the 1850s, nine to the 1860s, and six to either of those two decades. Additionally, I've assigned five to the latter part of the 1840s. This puts 90 percent of them in a 20-year period of 1848 to 1868. I've assigned three to the 1870s and one to the 1880s. I've found a few billboard-style slabs that were created in the 1870s and 1880s that were set on the ground in slotted bases instead of being elevated. Similar to billboards, they have multiple inscription panels for their family members. This tells me that in the latter part of the century, carvers had begun to recognize the fragility of these massive slabs and so they were bringing them back down to earth. The Mower family monument at Mount Auburn Cemetery in Auburn is a good example. It looks exactly like a billboard slab and it memorializes five children who died between 1878 and 1883. But, it is set into a slotted base on the ground.[23]

Material: 34 are marble, three are slate, and the missing Huse monument in Portland is of unknown stone but very likely was marble.

Support structures: 15 have pocket-slot granite posts, 12 have drop-slot granite posts, two are pinned to granite posts, three are held up by metal poles and clamps, three (probably four) are hooked onto posts, and two are metal-framed. Additionally, 15 have metal crossbar supports, 13 do not, eight are constructed such that a metal crossbar was not applicable to their design, and for two billboards it is unknown if they have one or not.

Makers: I originally thought that I'd find the billboard design to be the work of one midcentury marble worker. Instead, I

---

23. To see this monument, visit findagrave.com and search for Harry Mower, who died 1883.

found that there were at least six makers of these monuments. That billboards also exist elsewhere in New England suggests there were likely even more makers than I've been able to identify.

Health: The majority of Maine's billboards have condition issues. Twenty-three of them (60 percent of the total) have problems ranging from splayed posts and stress fractures to complete collapse and missing pieces.

The tables in the Appendix list the 38 Maine billboards found to date, by town. I invite anyone who finds one not already documented to be in touch with me via my Facebook page or by email (roroman@maine.rr.com).

The End?
(I can't imagine it really is…)

APPENDIX A

LOCATIONS OF BILLBOARD MONUMENTS IN MAINE

APPENDIX B

CONSTRUCTION DETAILS: MATERIAL, STRUCTURE, SIZE, AND WEIGHT. ORGANIZED BY TOWN

town	cemetery	family name	stone	support	metal crossbar	dimensions L x H x W	dry weight
Auburn	Plains	Leavitt	marble	drop-slot granite posts	no	32.75 x 23 x 2	140
Bridgton	High Street	Thompson	marble	metal poles with clamps	N/A	38 x 25.5 x 1.85	166
Bridgton	Sweden Road	Hazen	marble	metal poles with clamps	N/A	79.5 x 24 x 2	354
Bucksport	Riverview	Rich	marble	metal posts	N/A	52.75 x 18.75 x 1.6	146
Buxton	South Buxton	Elden	marble	pocket-slot granite posts	yes	41 x 17.5 x 4	265
Buxton	South Buxton	Lane	marble	pocket-slot granite posts	yes	45 x 16.75 x 2	140
Cumberland	Congregational	Blanchard	slate	granite posts w/ metal hooks	N/A	84 x 22.5 x 1.75	321
Cumberland	Congregational	Prince	marble	metal frame and hooks	N/A	72 x 24 x 2	320
Cumberland	Congregational	Sawyer	marble	granite posts w/ metal hooks	N/A	78 x 23 x 1.75	291
Dover-Foxcroft	Dover	Houston	marble	drop-slot granite posts	no	50 x 20 x 2	185
Garland	Burnham	Burnham	marble	drop-slot granite posts with metal clips	no	78 x 24 x 2	347

town	cemetery	family name	stone	support	metal crossbar	dimensions L x H x W	dry weight
Harrison	South Harrison	Jackson	marble	metal poles with clamps	N/A	70.5 x 24.75 x 2	323
Jackson	Jackson Corner	Warren	marble	drop-slot granite posts	yes	56 x 24.25 x 2	251
Jay	Beans Corner	Chandler	marble	pinned to granite posts	yes	53 x 16 x 2	157
Kennebunkport	Bass Cove	Foss-Goodwin	marble	drop-slot granite posts	no	73.5 x 29 x 2.125	419
Kennebunkport	Bass Cove	Tapley	marble	drop-slot granite posts	no	71.5 x 23.75 x 1.75	275
Kennebunkport	Bass Cove	Ward	marble	drop-slot granite posts	?	30 x 10.5 x 2	58
Livermore Falls	Shuy Yard	Pettingill	marble	pocket-slot granite posts	yes	60 x 24 x 2	267
Mount Vernon	Stevens	Thing	marble	pocket-slot granite posts	yes	57 x 23 x 3	364
Ogunquit	Riverside	Maxwell	marble	pocket-slot granite posts	yes	38 x 15 x 1.75	92
Poland	Locust	Glysson	slate	new wood braces	?	73 x 24 x 1.5	255
Poland	Locust	Schellinger	slate	granite posts with metal hooks	N/A	72 x 24 x 1.75	294
Portland	Eastern	Huse	?	pocket-slot granite posts	no	72 x 24 x 2	?
Prospect	Maple Grove	Mudgett	marble	drop-slot granite posts	yes	48 x 18.25 x 2	162
Ripley	Downing	Goodwin	marble	pocket-slot granite posts	yes	48 x 24 x ?	160 to 200

APPENDIX B *CONTINUED*

CONSTRUCTION DETAILS: MATERIAL, STRUCTURE, SIZE, AND WEIGHT. ORGANIZED BY TOWN

town	cemetery	family name	stone	support	metal crossbar	dimensions L x H x W	dry weight
Saco	Laurel Hill	Paul	marble	pocket-slot granite posts	no	71 x 24 x 1.75	276
Wells	Ocean View	Hill	marble	drop-slot granite posts	yes	45.5 x 26 x 1.75	192
Wells	Ocean View	Hubbard	marble	drop-slot granite posts	yes	38 x 18 x 1.75	111
Wells	Ocean View	Staples	marble	drop-slot granite posts	yes	38.5 x 16 x 1.75	100
Wilton	East Wilton	Butterfield	marble	pinned to granite posts	yes	42.5 x 18 x 2.25	160
Wilton	East Wilton	Smith	marble	pocket-slot granite posts	no	52.5 x 24 x 2	233
Wilton	Weld Street	Adams	marble	pocket-slot granite posts	no	48.5 x 20 x 2	180
Wilton	Weld Street	Hardy	marble	pocket-slot granite posts	yes	Each slab: 76 x 18 x 2.25	285
Wilton	Weld Street	Woodman	marble	pocket-slot granite posts	no	78 x 25.25 x 2	365
Yarmouth	Hillside	Hill	marble	pocket-slot granite posts	no	72 x 30 x 2	400
Yarmouth	Hillside	Sargent	marble	pocket-slot granite posts	no	84 x 28 x 2	436
York	First Parish	Trafton	marble	drop-slot granite posts	yes	60 x 17.5 x 2	194

APPENDIX C

DATES, MAKERS, AND CONDITION. ORGANIZED BY TOWN

town	cemetery	family name	date made	maker	condition
Auburn	Plains	Leavitt	1880s		OK
Bridgton	High Street	Thompson	1860s		OK
Bridgton	Sweden Road	Hazen	c. 1862		stress fracture, near clamp
Bucksport	Riverview	Rich	c. 1852		sliding into ground; lower small stress fracture
Buxton	South Buxton	Elden	c. 1876		OK
Buxton	South Buxton	Lane	1850s to 1860s		stress fracture, bottom center
Cumberland	Congregational	Blanchard	c. 1849		posts cracked at top where metal hooks are embedded; one post broken away, one with spider cracking
Cumberland	Congregational	Prince	c. 1849		OK
Cumberland	Congregational	Sawyer	c. 1849	Joseph R. Thompson, Portland	OK
Dover-Foxcroft	Dover	Houston	1850s to 1860s		OK

APPENDIX C *CONTINUED*

DATES, MAKERS, AND CONDITION. ORGANIZED BY TOWN

town	cemetery	family name	date made	maker	condition
Garland	Burnham	Burnham	c. 1863		posts cracked and repaired with metal collars; center support may be later (stone doesn't fit well in it)
Harrison	South Harrison	Jackson	c. 1861		stress fracture, near clamp
Jackson	Jackson Corner	Warren	c. 1858		sliding from left post
Jay	Beans Corner	Chandler	c. 1855		stress fracture, bottom left
Kennebunkport	Bass Cove	Foss-Goodwin	c. 1873		corner break, upper right panel
Kennebunkport	Bass Cove	Tapley	c. 1862		full break; posts are missing caps; photograph window empty
Kennebunkport	Bass Cove	Ward	c. 1857		OK
Livermore Falls	Shuy Yard	Pettingill	c. 1850		OK
Mount Vernon	Stevens	Thing	1866	William H. Rollins	leaning heavily; missing photo
Ogunquit	Riverside	Maxwell	1850s to 1860s		OK (Sonny Perkins conserved this BB in October 2019.)
Poland	Locust	Glysson	c. 1845		missing posts
Poland	Locust	Schellinger	c. 1848		OK

town	cemetery	family name	date made	maker	condition
Portland	Eastern	Huse	c. 1865		missing slab, only posts remain
Prospect	Maple Grove	Mudgett	c. 1855		OK
Ripley	Downing	Goodwin	1856	Baker, Emery & Co., Skowhegan	stress fracture, upper right
Saco	Laurel Hill	Cutts	c. 1855		OK
Saco	Laurel Hill	Paul	c. 1858		corner break, lower right
Wells	Ocean View	Hill	c. 1853		OK
Wells	Ocean View	Hubbard	1850s to 1860s		OK
Wells	Ocean View	Staples	1850s to 1860s		corner break, lower left
Wilton	East Wilton	Butterfield	1850s to 1860s		OK
Wilton	East Wilton	Smith	c. 1860	George W. Wise, Canton	stress fracture, small, bottom center
Wilton	Weld Street	Adams	c. 1863		unbroken but fallen; posts are splayed
Wilton	Weld Street	Hardy	c. 1879		OK

APPENDIX C *CONTINUED*

DATES, MAKERS, AND CONDITION. ORGANIZED BY TOWN

town	cemetery	family name	date made	maker	condition
Wilton	Weld Street	Woodman	c. 1858	Richard Smith, Dixfield	OK (slab seems sound) but the two outer posts in this chained family lot have fallen
Yarmouth	Hillside	Hill	1859	Hunt & Jewett, Portland	full break, center, and later repair includes placement of a center post immediately under the crack
Yarmouth	Hillside	Sargent	1853		stress fractures (3), along lower edge
York	First Parish	Trafton	c. 1864		full break (2), badly repaired

BIBLIOGRAPHY

Adams, Andrew N. *A Genealogical History of Robert Adams of Newbury, Mass., and His Descendants, 1635–1900.* Rutland, VT: The Tuttle Co., Printers, 1900.

Adams, George. *The Maine Register and Business Directory for the Year 1856.* South Berwick, ME: Edward C. Parks, 1856.

Bassett, Mary Cooley & Johnston, Sarah Hall. *Lineage Book, National Society of the DAR, vol. XL.* Washington, DC: 1915.

Bates, Joshua. *Sermon Delivered Before THE SOCIETY FOR PROPAGATING THE GOSPEL Among the Indians and Others in North America at their anniversary November 4, 1813.* Boston: 1813.

Batignani, Karen Wentworth. *Maine's Coastal Cemeteries: A Historic Tour.* Camden, ME: Down East Books, 2003.

Benes, Peter. *Additional Light on Wooden Grave Markers.* Essex Institute Historical Collections, Vol. 111—January 1975. Salem, MA: The Essex Institute, 1975.

The Board of Trade Journal, Vol. 23, 1910–1911.

Bourne, Edward E. *The History of Wells and Kennebunk.* Portland, ME: B. Thurston & Company, 1875.

Brooks, Annie Peabody. *Ropes' Ends.* Portland, ME: The Lakeside Press, 1901.

Burgess, Frederick. *English Churchyard Memorials.* London: Lutterworth Press, 1963.

Chandler, George. *The Chandler Family: The Descendants of William and Annis Chandler Who Settled in Roxbury, Mass. 1637.* Worcester, Mass: Press of Charles Hamilton, 1883.

Chapman, Jacob. *A Genealogy of the Folsom Family: John Folsom and His Descendants. 1615–1882.* Concord, NH: The Republican Press Association, 1882.

The Charter...Rules and Orders of the Common Council of the City of Portland. Portland, ME: The Argus Office, 1842.

Church, Jason. "Calculating the Weight of Stone." National Center for Preservation Technology and Training, www.ncptt.nps.gov, December 18, 2012.

Clayton, W. W. *History of Cumberland Co., Maine, With Illustrations and Biographical Sketches of Its Prominent Men and Pioneers.* Philadelphia: Everts & Peck, 1880.

Constitution and History of the Maine Charitable Mechanic Association. Portland, ME: Bryant Press, 1965.

Crowell, Elizabeth A. & Mackey, Norman Vardney III. *The Funerary Monuments and Burial Patterns of Colonial Tidewater Virginia, 1607–1776.* Markers VII. Greenfield, MA: Association for Gravestone Studies, 1990.

Davis, Walter Goodwin. *The Ancestry of Joseph Waterhouse 1754–1837 of Standish, Maine.* Portland, ME: The Anthoensen Press, 1949.

Davis, Walter Goodwin. *The Ancestry of Sarah Miller 1755–1840... of Arundel (Kennebunkport) Maine.* Portland, ME: The Southworth-Anthoensen Press, 1939.

DePeu, Rev. John. *Rural Cemeteries.* State of Connecticut Thirtieth Annual Report of the Secretary of the Connecticut Board of Agriculture, pp. 95–116. Hartford, CT: The Press of The Case, Lockwood & Brainard Company, 1897.

Drummond, Josiah H. *Joshua Bean of Exeter, Brentwood and Gilmanton, N. H. and Some of His Descendants.* Portland, ME: Smith & Sale, Printers, 1903.

Eaton, Priscilla. "The Barque Isidore of Kennebunk, Maine: Genealogy of a Shipwreck." *The Maine Genealogist,* Vol. 38, No. 2, May 2016.

Emery, George Addison. *Colonel Thomas Cutts: Saco's Most Eminent Citizen in the Country's Early Days.* Saco, ME: 1917.

Forman, Benno M. *A New Light on Early Grave Markers.* Essex Institute Historical Collections, Vol. CIV—1968. Salem, MA: The Essex Institute, 1968.

First Book of Records of the Town of Pepperellborough now the City of Saco. Portland, ME: The Thurston Press, 1896.

Granite, Marble & Bronze, Vol. XXVI, Number 1. Boston: January 1916.
Hardy, H. Claude & Noah, Rev. Edwin. *Hardy and Hardie Past and Present.* Syracuse, NY: The Syracuse Typesetting Co., Inc., 1935.

Harris, Samuel L. *The Maine Register and National Calendar for the Year 1843.* Augusta, ME: Daniel C. Stanwood, 1843.

Hoyt, Edmund S. *Maine State Year-Book, Annual Register for the Year 1871*. Portland, ME: Hoyt, Fogg & Breed, 1971.

Hubbard, Harlan Page. *One Thousand Years of Hubbard History 866 to 1895*. New York: G. W. Rodgers & Co, 1895.

Huse, Harry Pinckney. *The Descendants of Abel Huse of Newbury (1602–1690)*. Washington, DC: W. F. Roberts Co., 1935.

Jewett, Clayton E. *The Battlefield and Beyond: Essays on the American Civil War*. Baton Rouge: Louisiana State University Press, 2012.

Jewett, Frederic Clarke, M.D. *History and Genealogy of the Jewetts of America*. New York: The Grafton Press, 1908.

Jewett, Nathaniel G. *The Portland Directory & Register*. Portland, ME: Todd and Smith, 1823.

Jordan, William B., Jr. *Burial Records, 1717–1962 of the Eastern Cemetery, Portland, Maine*. Westminster, MD: Heritage Books, 2009.

Jordan, William B., Jr. *Eastern Cemetery, Portland, Maine: Record of Interments with Historical Notes*. Portland, ME: 1978.

Kewley, Jonathan. *Behind the Bedheads: The Earliest American Grave Markers and the Question of English Roots*. Markers XXXII. Greenfield, MA: Association for Gravestone Studies, 2016.

Kingsbury, Henry D. & Deyo, Simeon L. *Illustrated History of Kennebec County Maine*. New York: H.W. Blake & Company, 1892.

Lawrence, Rev. Benjamin F. *History of Jay, Franklin County, Maine*. Boston: Griffith-Stillings Press, 1912.

Lineage Book: National Society of the Daughters of the American Revolution, Jean Winslow Coltrane, Historian General. Volume LIX 1906, Washington, DC: 1922.

Lines Composed on the Loss of the Barque Isidore, of Kennebunkport... (unidentified author and publisher). Broadside #186, Collections of Maine Historical Society.

Making History: Art and Industry in the Saco River Valley (Saco Museum Exhibit Guide), J.S. McCarthy Printers, 2010.

Manning, William H. *The Genealogical and Biographical History of the Manning Families of New England and Descendants...* Salem, MA: The Salem Press Co., 1902.

The Marble Records Index and Locations of Cemeteries, Book No. 1, April 16, 1855 to November 10, 1856. Maine Old Cemetery Association, 2006.

Marshall, John A. *American Bastile. A History of the Illegal Arrests and Imprisonment of American Citizens During the Late Civil War.* Philadelphia: Thomas W. Hartley, 1874.

Material for a Genealogy of the Scammon Family in Maine. Salem, MA: The Salem Press, 1892.

Mitchell, Russell, & Strout. *The Cumberland and No. Yarmouth Register 1904.* Brunswick, ME: The H. E. Mitchell Pub. Co., 1904.

Mudgett, Mildred D. and Bruce D. *Thomas Mudgett of Salisbury, Massachusetts and His Descendants.* Bennington, VT: 1961.

New England Historical & Genealogical Register, V. 55. Boston: Published by the Society, 1901.

Norwood, Seth W. *Sketches of Brooks History.* Dover, NH: J.B. Page Printing Company, 1935.

Oak, Lyndon. *History of Garland, Maine.* Dover, ME: The Observer Publishing Company, 1912.

100 Years of Marriage and Divorce Statistics, United States, 1867–1967. DHEW Publication No. (HRA) 74-1902. Rockville, MD: December 1973.

Owen, Daniel E. *Old Times in Saco: A Brief Monograph on Local Events.* Saco, ME: 1891.

Palmer, Joseph. *Necrology of Alumni of Harvard College, 1851–52 to 1862–63.* Boston: John Wilson and Son, 1864.

Pease, Frederick S. *An Account of the Descendants of John Pease, Who Landed at Martha's Vineyard in the Year 1632.* Albany: Joel Munsell Printer, 1847.

Reid, Harvey. *The Wreck of the Isidore.* York, ME: Woodpecker Records, 2009.

The Reporter, Number 8. Chicago: August 1906.

Ricker, Alvan B., et al. *Poland Centennial September 11, 1895.* Poland, ME: Ricker, Fernald & Ricker, 1896.

Rounds, Leslie & Rounds, Emory. *Laurel Hill Cemetery of Saco, Maine.* Charleston, SC: The History Press, 2018.

Rowe, William H. *Ancient North Yarmouth and Yarmouth Maine, 1636–1936.* Portland, ME: The Southworth-Anthoensen Press, 1937.

Rust, Albert D. *Record of the Rust Family Embracing the Descendents of Henry Rust, who came from England and settled in Hingham, Mass., 1634–1635.* Waco, TX: Albert D. Rust, 1891.

The Sailor's Magazine and Naval Journal, Vol. XV, Ending August 1843. New York: American Seamen's Friend Society, J. F. Birch Printer, 1843.

Smith, Ned. *The 2nd Maine Cavalry in the Civil War: A History and Roster.* Jefferson, NC: McFarland Publishing, 2014.

Statistics of the United States in 1860; of the Eighth Census, Under the Direction of the Secretary of the Interior. Washington, DC: Government Printing Office, 1866.

Stinson, B. Craig. *A Brief History of Our Hill Family in America.* 2011.

Stocking, Rev. Charles Henry Wright. *The History and Genealogy of the Knowltons of England and America.* New York: The Knickerbocker Press, 1867.

Sweetser, Philip Starr. *Seth Sweetser and His Descendents.* Philadelphia: Integrity Press, 1938.

Town of Buxton, York County, ME Family Records, Book 4: Records of Births and Deaths, 1747–1887.

Transactions of the Maine Medical Association for the Years 1866, 1867, and 1868. Portland: Stephen Berry, Printer, 1869.

Vital Records of Sturbridge, Massachusetts, for the year 1850. Boston: New England Historic Genealogical Society, 1906.

Vital Statistics from the paper "Maine Farmer" for the period 1833 to 1852, Clarence A. Day, University of Maine.

Woodman, Cyrus. *The Woodmans of Buxton, ME.* Boston: David Clapp & Son, 1874.

GENERAL REFERENCES

Belfast Historical Society (Maine Memory Net on MHS)
Births and Deaths in Kennebunkport (Kennebunkport ME Town
    and Vital Records 1678–1891)
Buxton, Maine Historical Society
County Probate Offices throughout Maine
Eighth Maine Regiment Museum, Peaks Island, ME
Harvard University Student Directories
Maine Charitable Mechanic Association Library Collections
Maine Maritime Museum: Historical Notes
Maine Register and Business Directories
Maine Vital Records (various sources)
New York City Municipal Deaths, 1795–1949 database
Portland, ME, City Directories
South Carolina Historical Society
Town of Wells, York County Maine, Record of Births, Deaths
    and Marriages, 1770 to 1810
US Census Collection
US National Archives/Civil War
Yarmouth, ME, Historical Society

WEBSITES

amlinkmarble.com
ancestry.com
findagrave.com
familysearch.org
genealogybank.org
newspapers.com

INDEX (BY CATEGORY)

Towns with Billboards

Cemeteries with Billboards

FAMILY NAMES

MONUMENT MAKERS

General Topics Index

ABOUT THE AUTHOR

*R*on Romano was raised in Portland, Maine, and spent his college and career years in Boston. After receiving a master's degree in Public Health Administration, he became a vice president at an insurance company and an adjunct professor teaching graduate students about managed health care. As exciting as that sounds, Ron retired early and moved back to Maine. He serves on the board of *Spirits Alive* (a local organization, the Friends of Portland's Historic Eastern Cemetery), managing its popular walking tours program, and on the board of the *Association for Gravestone Studies* (a national organization) helping to improve the organization's effectiveness. He's a frequent lecturer on Maine's gravestone makers, symbolism, and historic cemeteries. His perfect day includes coffee, a cemetery stroll, bird-watching, pasta, and a movie. And chocolate. This is Ron's third gravestone- and cemetery-themed book.